The Identity of
Jesus of Nazareth

CARL F. H. HENRY

The
IDENTITY OF
JESUS
OF
NAZARETH

BROADMAN PRESS
NASHVILLE, TENNESSEE

4215-46

ISBN: 0-8054-1546-7

Dewey Decimal Classification: 232
Subject Heading: CHRISTOLOGY // JESUS CHRIST
Library of Congress Catalog Number: 92-10622
Printed in the United States of America
All Scripture quotations are the author's translation.

Library of Congress Cataloging-in-Publication Data

Henry, Carl Ferdinand Howard, 1913-
    The identity of Jesus of Nazareth / Carl F.H. Henry.
    p. cm.
    Includes bibliographical references.
    ISBN 0-8054-1546-7
    1. Jesus Christ—Person and offices. I. Title.
BT202.H433 1991
232—dc20

92-10622
CIP

Contents

Part 1

The Identity of
Jesus of Nazareth

1

Disparate Views of Jesus

Nowhere is the tension between historically repeatable acts and a once-for-all event focused more dramatically than in the conflict over the identity of Jesus of Nazareth. Shall we explain him as the ideal model of mankind and expound divine incarnation by philosophical analysis of what is humanly possible, or shall we depict him rather in terms of the christologically unparalleled?

The Gospels provide our only significant information about Jesus' life and work. Skeptical critics thrust upon these sources tests of reliability that they do not impose upon other historical writing. If universally applied, those same criteria would in principle invalidate ancient Greek and Roman accounts that secular historians routinely accept as factual (cf. Sherwin-White, 1963).

Efforts to destroy the credibility of the Gospels often betray a bias against the supernatural. Gerald G. O'Collins (1987: vol. 8, p. 266) recalls "the official Soviet thesis (which appears recently to have been abandoned) that Jesus never existed and was a purely mythological figure." Consistent Marxists would need to reject the theology-of-revolution view that the historical figure of Jesus nurtures its liberationist challenge to an alienated world. The assumptions of evolutionary naturalism likewise lead to a rejection of Jesus as in any way normative and decisive for human destiny.

Jesus in the Views of Other World Religions

Jewish Views of Jesus

The New Standard Jewish Encyclopedia (ed. Cecil Roth and Geoffrey Wigoder, 1975:1042) escapes the larger question of the significance of Jesus by a generalized comment that "certain sections [of the Gospels] seem to reflect ideas and situations in the developing Christian church rather than those of Jesus' own day." Were the editors to apply this complaint consistently to all the biblical data, they would need to devalue also the Old Testament whose reliability they assume. Curiously, whenever these same editors charge the Evangelists with "anti-Jewish sentiment" they accept the Gospels as accurate representations of the Evangelists' sentiments.

The controversy over the identity and importance of Jesus arose initially in the context of Hebrew history and religion. This spiritual community devoutly expected a messianic deliverer, an expectation grounded in Yahweh's special prophetic revelation. The Jewish community divided in Jesus' day over Jesus' messianic role. The Gospels detail the conflict among Jesus' religious contemporaries over whether to receive or to repudiate the Nazarene as the promised Messiah and divine Son of God.

The Christian church was at its beginning overwhelmingly Jewish in composition. Jews were faced by a choice that the New Testament still thrusts upon its readers, whether to affirm Jesus' divinity or to repudiate him as a blasphemer and messianic pretender. Simply to honor him as humanity at its best was not an option.

But modern critical thought sought to eviscerate the messianic eschatology of Jesus, even his Jewishness, and to obscure his life, resurrection and ascension, and turned him instead, as Stanley Hauerwas says, into a teacher of noble ideals, "the pinnacle of the highest and best in humanity... civilization's very best." "It was a short step," Hauerwas adds, "from the biblical Christ—the highest in humanity—to the Nazi Superman" (1989:25).

Antagonists of the first four centuries (A.D.) dismissed Jesus as either a deceiver or a megalomaniac. *Toledot Yeshu* and other early Talmudic stories cast aspersions on Jesus' origin and character. Presuming to speak for most present-day Jews, rabbi Yachiel Eckstein contends that Jesus was merely "another martyred Jew, one of the many false prophets and pseudo-messiahs" (1984:242).

In striking contrast, some recent Jewish leaders unhesitatingly applaud the man Jesus. Even the Jewish rebel Spinoza (1632-77), while disavowing the divinity of Christ, nonetheless considered Jesus the greatest and noblest of all prophets (*Epistle* 21). C. G. Montefiore (1858-1925) and Joseph Klausner (1874-1960) paid Jesus notable tribute. Montefiore significantly commended Jesus over the whole talmudic inheritance: "We certainly do not get in the Hebrew Bible any teacher speaking of God as 'Father,' 'my Father,' 'your Father,' and 'our Father' like the Jesus of Matthew." He writes, "We do not get so habitual and concentrated a use [of Father for God] from any Rabbi in the Talmud" ([1923] 1972:205). Many writers not victimized by a skeptical view of history now readily concede that Jesus towers above the stream of mankind as an individual of rare spiritual sensitivity, devotion, and compassion.

In the book *The Jewish Reclamation of Jesus*, Donald A. Hagner acknowledges that most contemporary Jewish scholarship and Jewish-Christian dialogue still reflects long-standing differences from the evangelical view of Jesus. But he considers "remarkable and significant" the current extensive Jewish research and the evidence it gives of "a drastic change in the Jewish appreciation of Jesus" (1984:273). To be sure, the Jewish theological stance remains hostile to the Christian doctrines of incarnation, atonement, and the Trinity, and it refuses to connect Jesus with any significant transformation of the world-order and any new and decisive historical inbreaking of the Kingdom of God. Yet careful reading of the Gospels increasingly overcomes the ready complaint that Christianity is anti-Semitic, and it more and more elicits a sporadic acknowledgment of their claims to historical trustworthiness, as does Pinchas Lapide's admission of the resurrection of Jesus. Alongside this may be noted the clusters of secret believers in the state of Israel, and the remarkable conversion to Christ of many Jews in other lands. It is safe to say that tens of thousands of modern Jews affirm that Jesus fulfills the Old Testament prophecies and is "the Christ, the Son of the living God" (Matt 16:16).

Ironically, as David Novak observes, some Jewish thinkers have judged Islam more favorably than Christianity because of Islam's supposedly stricter monotheism and absolute prohibition of images, in contrast with Christian trinitarianism and the use of images in worship by some major branches of Christianity (1991:28). In the later Middle Ages, however, Jews took a more positive view, one that judged Christianity not idolatrous and which acknowledged trinitarianism to be not necessarily a commitment to a different God than Yahweh.

Islamic Views of Jesus

Despite its nontrinitarian theology, the Koran nevertheless distinguishes Jesus from the rest of humanity by affirming his virgin birth, sinlessness, messianity, and ascension to heaven prior to the endtime resurrection of all humanity. The Koran portrays Jesus as Word of God (*Kalimah*), even if it does so in less than orthodox Christian terms. To be sure, Islam declares Jesus to be "merely *a* prophet, *a* sent one, *a* word" and thus excludes his divinity, whereas the Christian revelation affirms him to be *the* Sent One, *the* incarnate Word. Some Muslims assuredly welcome as a constructive contribution to interreligious dialogue only christological affirmations that preclude divine incarnation in Christ.

Yet it is all too easy, as Thomas O'Shaughnessy remarks, to level Muhammad's view of Jesus to that of simply another human being, and to ignore his intimation of a considerably higher view (1948:15). One could in fact "construct a rudimentary Life of Christ," remarks F. P. Cotterell, from the reference to Jesus (Isa) in the Koran, although some materials, e.g., childhood miracles attributed to him, have an apocryphal rather than biblical basis (1982:282). Muhammad claims, of course, that the entire content of the Koran came as a divine revelation from the Preserved Tablet and not from earthly sources. It is unlikely that an Arabic version of the Gospels was available to him, and orally circulating late tradition could readily have mixed fact and legend.

While the New Testament calls Jesus Son of God twenty-five times and Son of Mary only once, the Koran uses the title Son of Mary twenty-three times. The Koran is less explicit than the New Testament on the subject of Mary's virginity, although it does not preclude this and even implies it. The Koran affirms that the conception of Jesus was through the Word of God (Sura 3:47).

Yet, as Cotterell notes, the Koran is not much interested in the events of Jesus' earthly life and ministry. We are told that Jesus had disciples and performed miracles. Alongside New Testament sources, however, the Koranic account seems often slurred and confused. The most striking difference is the Koranic notion that Jesus did not die upon the cross (Sura 4:157). The conventional interpretation is that he was translated into heaven without crucifixion and that another person replaced him (one fanciful theory nominates Judas). A rival interpretation alleges that he was impaled on the cross but did not die there; supposedly recovering in the tomb, he escaped to Kashmir where he subsequently died. In either case the Koran here is at odds with all historical scholarship. As Geoffrey Parrinder remarks, "No serious modern historian doubts that Jesus... was crucified, whatever he may think of the faith or the resurrection" (1977:116). Even in respect to this major historical event the Koran therefore shows itself to be less than a trustworthy guide. Parrinder discusses E. E. Elder's suggestion that we interpret the Koran to mean that Jesus' death upon the cross was a divine act, not a human act (1977:119-21). But this is unhelpful, since in that event the significance of Jesus' passion is wholly ignored.

Jesus in the Views of Contemporary Theology and Philosophy

When we speak of Jesus, do we then nonetheless in fact deal simply with a man who like other founders of religions made unique claims about genuine spiritual experience? Or with a notably inspired and inspiring prophet who confronts us with a specially lively sense of the supernatural? Or a man through whom God superlatively manifested himself, and perhaps performed works unmatched in human history? These questions have been answered in numerous ways.

Manifold Views of Jesus

Most, if not all, of these contemporary views, regardless of how honorific, do not conclusively modify a perspective that begins and ends with man. Is Jesus then only an ancient Semite that literary embellishment has lifted from an obscure life on the outposts of Hellenistic-Roman civilization?

Or is he merely a devout Jew engaged in a dispute with fellow Jews over the proper interpretation of Judaism? Is he but a Christian alternative to the Hellenic savior-gods, one fashioned by miracle stories set in a Palestinian Semitic context?

Was Jesus of Nazareth, as Jane Schabert declares, a biologically natural son born to Mary through rape or seduction in a disgraceful paternity that the Gospel accounts turn to glory (1987)? Is Jesus the *Wunderkind* of the apocryphal Gospels, a child genius who worked miracles even while at play?

Is he an itinerant Galilean Semite imaginatively sharing his people's apocalyptic hopes, or as Nietzsche contended ([1930] 1972), simply a dread-filled hypersensitive type, a religiously obsessed fanatic warning us of the End of all ends?

Is he a contemplative sage offering words of wisdom as did Confucius, Socrates, and Epictetus, a majestic guru imparting universal truths about life and mortality? Was he, as speculative psychologists have suggested, extraordinarily endowed with extra-sensory perception? Is he the prophet of the "New Age" consciousness, a model of human insights creatively open to depths of divinity in one's own inner selfhood? Does he transcend the merely human as an historical presence that discloses our overlooked possibilities and enlivens our imaginative powers? Is he an invisible comrade, the lively memory of whose earthly example still supplies inspiration and courage for the facing of life's problems?

Shall we say with Paul Van Buren, that Jesus is "the perfect embodiment of divine love" (1980:118)? Was he so venerated that his colleagues could not believe that he was dead? Is he, as Rudolf Bultmann viewed him, a man whose crucifixion cut short his earthly life but who in the church's proclamation became God and accumulated such aspects of supernatural mythology as virgin birth, incarnation, atonement, resurrection, and ascension? Is he merely a literary fiction of the Gospel Evangelists, a mythical depiction that externalizes and objectifies an inner experience of new being? Is he rather, as Gnostics held, the phantasmal appearance that illuminates the dark world of a supreme but otherwise unknowable God? Does he, as Paul Tillich put it, stand in complete relational participation with the Ground of all Being (1951-63:2:148)?

Is the term "Christ" simply a semantic symbol for whatever satisfies human craving for a fuller life, and hence an expression serviceable to atheists and materialists as well as to biblical Christians? Does he exhibit human nature at its best, as at once the restorer of authentic humanity, and the consummator of mankind? Is he the ethical norm by whose example humans in all generations must measure virtue? Shall we with John A. T. Robinson say that he is a complete embodiment "of what was from the beginning the meaning and purpose of God's self-expression," a human person who "embodied the divine initiative and saving presence so completely that he was declared at his baptism and confirmed at his resurrection to be everything God himself was" (1973:77, 162)? Is he, as Piet Schoonenberg portrays him, the ultimate of human-ness in whose person we find God's complete presence (1971:7, 136)? Is Hans Kung right, that Jesus "*represents the permanently reliable* ultimate standard of human existence" (1976:443)?

Is he, as L. S. Thornton suggested, founder of a new humanity that towers above mankind today even as *homo sapiens* now transcends the lower animal creation (1928:35, 367-68). Is he a super-Apollo, a spiritual athlete, as Renaissance art at times seems to depict him in a mediating effort to gain a Christian advantage from emerging humanism? Is he, as Pierre Teilhard de Chardin avers, the focus of cosmic evolution as its final unification and "christification" of all reality? Or is he the "political Christ"—the prophet of social revolution and catalyst for the revolutionary overthrow of social structures—as Gustavo Gutierrez would have it (1973)? Must we, in contrast to early Latin credal christology, accommodate current Latin American alternatives like the "charismatic Christ" and the "guerilla Christ"? Is he a social humanitarian concerned for liberation of the working class, a defender of lesser landholders against their landlords?

Is Jesus, as W. Pannenberg holds, not a virgin's son, but nonetheless by his resurrection attested as the eternal Son of God and manifest thereby as preexistently sharing the divine essence (1977:156,353)? Is Jesus, as Oscar Cullman concedes, not only the sinless bearer of messianic self-consciousness, but one whose deity we properly affirm in view of God's distinctive revelatory activity through him, yet concerning whose divine essence and dual natures it is useless to speculate (1963:93,266,277,306)?

This incomplete sampling of current views of the Nazarene, remarkable for its disagreements, leaves little doubt that modernity has blurred Jesus into history's most displaced person. In a recent book, *Jesus Through the Centuries: His Place in the History of Culture* (1986), Jaroslav Pelikan reflects the many diverse images and cultural understandings of Jesus through which the biblical portrait tends to lose normative theological significance. Alfred Rosenberg, the Nazi movement's official philosopher, even held that Jesus could not have been a Jew, but depicted him rather as a Nordic anti-Semite (cf. Morris, 1983:82). So multiform are the views of the Nazarene that an atheist is said to have jeered that "there is no god, and Jesus is his problem." As Douglas Groothuis says, "No other name has inspired greater devotion, evoked greater reverence, or ignited greater controversy" (1990:9).

Must we then concede with Albert Schweitzer that the historical Jesus is "to our time a stranger and enigma" (1910:396)? Or must we rather remind our generation of the baneful influence of alien speculative theories? Respectful mention of Jesus' name embarrasses much of our secular society. A liberal elite is prone to avoid introduction of the Nazarene as socially disruptive. The mass media seem at times to reserve the name of Jesus for use only in profanity. Yet serious discussion of the significance of the Nazarene cannot be removed from the contemporary agenda. The twentieth-century space age has set the discussion of Christ in the near-neighbor context of Buddhists, Hindus, and Muslims who press the question of Jesus' identity even if some Christians prefer to suppress it.

Many scholars who reject the Chalcedonian formulation

that Jesus is true God and true man, and who instead hold to a one-nature view of Jesus, nonetheless distinguish him from the entirety of the human race. Tributes paid to Jesus even by scholars who disavow the historic christological creeds not only revere the Nazarene above his contemporaries, but elevate him as well above all human beings ancient and modern. These assessments of Jesus Christ exhaust ordinary anthropological categories in explanation of him. In contrast to the inherited view of Jesus Christ as the full revelation of God in the flesh, Teilhard de Chardin holds that "Christ is not yet fully formed" (1961:133) and that he will not be until we are united in co-creative union with the Eucharistic Cosmic Christ" 1960:131-32). The universal Christ-idea or Christ-principle seems more important to Teilhard than is the Jesus of history. As James M. Houston comments, "Teilhard makes much of the cosmic Christ, but has little to say of the incarnate Christ" (1980:170). Yet students of the life of Jesus repeatedly refuse to dwarf him simply to a superman like Alexander the Great, Napoleon Bonaparte, or Winston Churchill, or to a superguru like Gandhi.

A Growing New Consensus

Any attentive reader of the Gospels will soon discover that the founder of the Christian religion differs greatly from the representations even of many philosophers, religious commentators, and social reformers who pay the Nazarene quite lofty compliments. He is, as Os Guinness reminds us, neither "the gentle Jesus meek and mild" as many project him, nor the theatrical "'Jesus Christ Superstar' with his tortured doubts and personality problems.... Such views... are not borne out by the objective evidence of the life of Christ.... The radical Christ of Pasolini's film *The Gospel According to St. Matthew*, the socialist Christ of much liberal activism, the Hindu Christ—these are not so much anti-Christian as unhistorical" (1973:355-56). The insistent Gospel witness to Jesus has, in fact, repeatedly made itself felt over against skeptical, imaginative, and mythical portrayals that rashly discount the New Testament writings.

"Surely," as Robert F. Berkey remarks, "no issues of Christian thought have gone through more thorough analyses in this century than those problems pertaining to the New Testament affirmations of the unique, unprecedented, once-for-all character of the person of Jesus" (1982:3). The outcome, moreover, contends Berkey, is that the theological climate has radically changed: a century that began with "no clear consensus" now insists that in any attempt to understand New Testament faith we must give full weight to christological affirmations and to the "once for all significance of the person of Christ" (ibid., 22).

In 1913 Wilhelm Bousset presumed to set forth in *Kyrios Christos* "a history of belief in Christ from the beginnings of Christianity to Irenaeus." Bousset projected a pre-Pauline Hellenistic Christian community that differed from Palestinian Jewish Christians by affirming a supernatural miraculous Jesus who was to be worshiped. On Palestinian soil and in Semitic context, Bousset held, Jesus was invoked simply as 'Master.' Only later, in Gentile context and under the influence of the Hellenistic savior-cults, was Jesus acclaimed as 'Lord.'

This view bequeaths as its "fundamental problem," as Hendrikus Boers observes, the notion that New Testament christology must be considered "not historically true of Jesus himself," so that the New Testament ceases to express "the truth about the historical Jesus" (1970:452).

Bousset sought to escape the devastating theological implications of this emphasis by contending that Jesus' teaching survives as a distinctive truth about God even when divested of certain later accretions. But Rudolf Bultmann more thoroughly applied the view that New Testament christology is a product of early Christianity. Bultmann disavowed entirely any reliable historical portrait of Jesus and declared the Gospels to be merely an expression of human self-understanding (1958). Herbert Braun dissolved New Testament Christology into an understanding of man mutually held by Jesus, the apostles, and the earthly church, one that loses any special knowledge of Jesus in a general anthropological outlook (1957:341-77; 1962:243-82).

Whatever we must in fact affirm about Jesus of Nazareth, his human nature must in no way be essentially impaired. The Christian doctrine of divine incarnation centers in a specific individual born in Bethlehem, reared in Nazareth, and crucified in Jerusalem. Whatever else the New Testament view of incarnation may require, the central figure of the Christian faith was during his earthly ministry, as Paul wrote Timothy, nothing less than "the man Christ Jesus" (1 Tim 2:5). No theory can be squared with the biblical doctrine of incarnation if it regards Jesus as an intermediate being, a demigod distinct from mankind. Nor is the notion acceptable that God merely assumed human disguise, the semblance of humanity, or even the suggestion that God for three decades merely adopted a human body and indwelt it as divine mind or spirit inhabiting a human physique. Nor is divine incarnation merely a superlative example of God indwelling mankind universally. It involves nothing less than a singular relationship of God to human nature without precedent or parallel in the realm of being or in the history of thought.

The modernist allegation that any affirmation of the divinity of Jesus Christ necessarily involves an obliteration of his humanity was already widely propagated in the closing decades of the nineteenth century. Adolf von Harnack deplored suppression of the real historical Jesus by the "fictitious" preexistent Christ (1909:1:704-05). Harnack defined the essence of Christianity as an agenda of moral and spiritual values that Jesus the teacher had stipulated.

To preserve Christ's full humanity, John Caird, in his end-of-the-century Gifford Lectures on *The Fundamental Ideas of Christianity* (1895-1896), insisted that Christ's divinity "was capable of being expressed in a human life and through the words and acts of a human personality." "Whatever of Divinity could not...breathe through a human spirit," said Caird, "could not be present in one who...was really and truly human." Christ's divinity was that "of a divine nature that suffused, blended, identified itself with the thoughts, feelings, volitions of a human individual" (Vol. 1:14). The result was an emphasis not on two natures united in one person, but on Christ's unitary *nature*, and a redefinition of Christ's divinity basically in terms of unbroken human-divine union.

This formulation inadequately states what the New Testament signifies by the deity of Christ. As John Stuart Lawton notes, it is merely an embellished unitarianism; it affirms the humanity of Christ's nature and personality yet disallows speaking of him as "personally God" (1947:313).

Somewhat similar was the view of William Temple, who found Christ's deity in his unity of purpose and harmonious willing with the Father (1934:445-46). H. R. Mackintosh hailed this view as a great theological advance (1913 [reprint 1942]:297). But one cannot logically categorize a human being as intrinsically divine simply because he perfectly obeys the will of God, since unbroken obedience was God's intention for all humanity at the creation. An honorifically-conferred divinity fails to affirm the unparalleled metaphysical unity of Father and Son that the New Testament asserts; instead, it accommodates unitarian theism. In the apostolic witness, as Lawton remarked,

> We do not simply find...a primarily moral man living a life in harmony with the will of God; in fact...we are told singularly little about Christ's thoughts or relationships in which a man's moral character is most clearly displayed. We are presented with a figure who, in the first place, possesses and exercises divine powers—he performs miracles of healing, control over nature, and superhuman vision: above all, he enters and leaves the world in a manner in which other men cannot. This figure, moreover, makes far-reaching claims for himself: he can remit the eternal guilt of sin, he proclaims himself equal with God, and foretells that he himself will sit as judge over all men at the grand assize (1943:323).

Despite its deep ecclesial inroads, modernistic theology failed to stifle transcendent Christology. Modernism's christological inconsistency Lawton traced to a vulnerable and indeed "wrong starting-point." "In the realm of pure Christology," he commented, it is "inexcusable...to begin with Christ's humanity and human life, and...to work upwards...to the confession of his Deity. Those who do not begin with the fundamental Christian assumption that 'the Word was made flesh,' but...attempt to show how...a complete man as they suppose Christ to have been was united to God" cannot but end in confused and self-contradictory views (ibid., 323-24).

Early repudiation of the modernist Jesus came not only from evangelical-orthodox expositors but on the one hand from faith-versus-reason champions of Christ's divinity paced by Soren Kierkegaard, Karl Barth, and Emil Brunner, and on the other from humanists who stressed the irreconcilability of liberal claims for Jesus' uniqueness with the scientific method which modernism professed to champion.

Kierkegaard affirmed that Christianity's towering truth—the incarnation—prompts a leap of faith that appropriates its consequences in life. By depicting the incarnation—the one solitary man Jesus Christ who is simultaneously the eternal God—as a paradox beyond the grasp of reason, Kierkegaard went beyond the early church fathers. When they wrote of the incarnation as a paradox, they did not disavow all rational comprehension of its reality. By connecting God's incarnation in Christ with a sheer leap of faith to which logical tests are irrelevant, Kierkegaard needlessly sacrificed the cognitive criteria that could invalidate unacceptable religious alternatives to Christian beliefs.

Barth also unqualifiedly affirmed the divinity of Christ as the eternal Word made flesh. He sharply contrasted the Son's relation to the Father with the saints' relation to God and decisively rejected the modernist emphasis on moral obedience as a complete definition of Jesus' divinity. To be sure, Barth's commendation also of the divinity of Scripture and of church proclamation (neither of which he considered infallible) raises problems, as does his insistence that the Logos assumed fallen human nature. Yet Barth waved aside contemporary theologians who first of all view Jesus as a Palestinian Jew, as do Caird and Temple and, more recently, Pannenberg. Charles Waldrop considers Barth's view Alexandrian rather than Antiochene in that he affirmed Jesus Christ to be essentially and by nature divine rather than merely a fully human individual who can also be declared divine (1981: 263). In line with this approach Sir Edwyn Hoskyns and Noel Davey likewise stress that the divinity of Jesus Christ is the forefront emphasis of the New Testament (1931).

While neo-orthodoxy turned to the Bible to vindicate its claims that modernism is a heretical deviation from the central witness of the Scriptures, naturalistic humanism struck at modernism from the left. Modernism had declared evangelical Christianity prescientific and antiscientific in view of its insistence on miraculous supernaturalism. Modernism replaced the divine Christ by the human Jesus viewed as humanity's moral exemplar. Modernism held, in short, that following the example of Jesus' superlative devotion to the Father ideally will deliver one from inner tension and discord to an integrated personality. To the humanist the modernist regard for Jesus as the sole spiritual catalyst conflicts with the tentative nature of empirical observation and with the assumption that other persons and even other causes may achieve the same ends. Modernism no less than evangelicalism, the humanists protested, applied scientific method and testing only in a limited way that prejudiced its christology. It was neither modernism nor neoorthodoxy that increasingly permeated secular university education, but rather humanism, which looked upon Jesus at best as an outstanding religious leader.

Less than a half century after Harnack and other European modernists declared orthodox christology *passe*, the World Council of Churches at its organizing assembly in Amsterdam in 1948 affirmed that Jesus Christ is "God and Savior." Although vulnerable to existential and perspectival deployment, the formulation placed christological concerns once again near the heart of ecumenical faith-and-order interests. The question was again insistently raised: May not Jesus of Nazareth, after all, be the Son of God and promised Messiah, God-beside-God, God come in the flesh in the stupendous miracle of divine incarnation?

2

The Gospels' Witness to Jesus

As noted above, the Gospels, which provide our only significant information about Jesus' life and work, detail the conflict among Jesus' religious contemporaries over whether to receive or to repudiate the Nazarene as the promised Messiah and divine Son of God. The New Testament still thrusts upon its readers the choice of whether to affirm Jesus' deity or not.

Messianic Self-Consciousness

What role has Jesus' own self-consciousness in respect to affirmations of his divinity? Unless the substance of the claims made by early Christianity can be legitimately referred back not to Jesus' contemporaries only, but also to what Jesus affirmed about himself, christology is in jeopardy. Christianity cannot persuasively claim for Jesus what he did not and does not claim for himself. This does not mean, of course, that the apostles through the guidance of the Spirit did not tell us more about Jesus' identity and accomplishments than he himself did (see John 16:12-15). We may have no access to Jesus' self-consciousness except through his words and acts as reflected in the Gospel records, but neglect of data concerning Jesus' own self-consciousness will obscure the contribution made by his own life and teaching to the attitude of the first Christians toward him.

All the Gospels contain passages in which Jesus affirmed or strongly implied his deity (e.g., Matt 11:27; Mark 2:5,10; 12:37; Luke 10:22; John 16:14-15; 14:26; 15:26; 16:7). The weight of the evidence is that Jesus believed that he was and is God's incomparable Son, standing in God's place with divine authority and right, and determining the destiny of

23

human beings according to their response to his life and work. Herbert Brown nonetheless declares it "probable" that Jesus lacked any messianic self-understanding (1979:26).

The challenge to the divinity of Jesus Christ in the second decade of this century was projected on the ground that the historical Jesus of the Synoptic Gospels made no supernatural claims for himself. But this contention crumbled under research showing that Jesus depicted himself as the Messiah of prophetic promise and that he implied a unique relationship not only to mankind but to God (cf. Manson, 1943). Burton Scott Easton remarked that "too many moderns treat" Jesus' messianic self-consciousness "as if it were something almost any religious man might possess," e.g., the fervent conviction that in the future judgment of the world one would "not be on man's side but on God's" (1928:160), which would in any other figure have aroused countercharges of delusion. Leonard Hodgson stressed that what Jesus "thought of Himself involves, if it be true, such a supernatural office as justifies the beliefs about him stated in the Christian creeds, and that if these elements in His thought are set on one side, whatever remains is not the historic Jesus" (1928:67).

Oscar Cullmann does not hesitate to affirm that Jesus Christ believed himself to be Messiah (1963:314-17). Prior to the Easter-experience both "Jesus' own self-consciousness" and "his person and work" provided a starting point of christological thought. Cullman notes, "From the moment of his baptism Jesus was conscious of carrying out God's plan" (1963:317).

As already mentioned in passing, Pannenberg considers the early Church the source of all the christological titles ascribed to Jesus; the titles therefore, as he sees it, do not directly attest Jesus' consciousness of unique unity with God. Pannenberg's rejection of the christological significance of the titles reflects the influence of questionable theological assumptions and prejudgment. The ontological structure of Jesus' divine-human consciousness he connects with a progressively developing self-understanding in intimate community with the Father's revelational presence, rather than with a Logos consciousness. While Pannenberg seeks to protect Jesus' sinlessness, he denies that he was free from error.

Jesus erred, says Pannenberg, by expecting the arrival of God's Kingdom in his own generation (1977:226). This lack of knowledge extended additionally to his own person. His complete dependence on and unity with God, with whose will he was functionally one in pre-actualizing the coming Kingdom, did not presuppose a messianic self-consciousness (1977:334). Yet Pannenberg holds that Jesus' sinlessness was a consequence not of incarnation in a specially purified humanity that constituted him incapable of sin; it presupposes rather that Jesus assumed sinful flesh existentially structured by self-centeredness, but that his resurrection attests that he conquered sin under the very conditions of human existence in bondage to sin (1977:354-56).

Jesus' personal community with the Father defines him as the Son of God. The resurrection of Jesus attests that God's will to establish the Kingdom governed his life and work. God raised Jesus as the One who in his mission was unreservedly dedicated to him and who self-sacrificially remained so dedicated even amid the seeming failure of that mission. Pannenberg maintains that the End (whose nearness Jesus proclaimed) did not come in the way in which Jesus and his disciples expected—the appearance of the heavenly Son of Man, universal resurrection of the dead, the last judgment—but rather in the manner of Jesus' own singular proleptic resurrection (ibid.).

Karl Rahner affirms that Jesus "knew he was indissolubly united with his God" (1974:158). Pannenberg, like Rahner, holds that Jesus' reflective messianic self-consciousness was an aspect of his personal intellectual history, and not due to an intrinsic and historically unconditioned awareness of the divine Logos. Jesus' self-knowledge arises in relation to the Father rather than to the Logos. Pannenberg regards the Hebrew religious heritage as crucial, particularly its emphasis on the nearness of the Kingdom of God. Jesus lacked complete preknowledge, even about his own person, although he knew himself to be functionally one with God's will (1977:334), and knew his ego to be other than that of the Father. Jesus' personal community with the Father identifies him as the Son of God, and the resurrection confirms his whole activity to be in dedication to God's purpose to estab-

lish the Kingdom. Pannenberg contends that as human existence gains integrated personality through dependence on
God the Father, Jesus too received his life-integrating personality in personal communion with the Father (1977:345).
In the revelation of Jesus as the Son of God, Pannenberg
finds Jesus' ultimate identification with the Lordship of God,
and hence his entry into kingly rule over all creation in
extension of God's Kingdom (1977:365), his headship of humanity as an aspect of cosmic reconciliation, and his eschatological consummation of the world and historical process.
Although Pannenberg does not regard salvation as automati-
cally universal, he nonetheless considers universal salvation
a theological option (1977:271-72).

James D. G. Dunn holds that much as one must acknowledge that Jesus claimed to be "the eschatological prophet"
and to speak as "the final envoy of Wisdom, with an immedi-
acy of revelatory authority that transcended anything that
had gone before...there is no indication that Jesus thought
or spoke of himself as having preexisted with God prior to his
birth or appearance on earth" (1980:253-56). But this verdict
can be achieved only by dismissing such texts as John 8 and
John 17 as late forms of tradition that cannot be traced back
to Jesus.

C. F. D. Moule is reluctant to find in Jesus' own consciousness an awareness of divine preexistence, a hesitancy that
seems strange in view of John 17:5 ("and now, O Father,
glorify Me with the glory which I had with you before the
world was"). Yet he retains the idea of Jesus' preexistence
and thinks that John (in 1:1-18) and Paul (in Col 1:15-17)
drew out "the implications of their experience of him as
transcending the temporal" (1977:138-39). This inference
centered especially, Moule thinks, in their relation to Jesus
as one who, beyond crucifixion, had without waiting for the
end of history entered into absolute life. Thus the Easter-
belief of the disciples that Jesus had passed through death
into "life absolute, life eternal" is for Moule the decisive
factor in affirming Jesus' supratemporal existence.

It is one thing to say, as Bultmann did, that Christology is
the creative invention of the post-crucifixion Christian community, and very much another thing to say, as does Moule,

that the resurrection-event congealed the latent Christian conviction of Jesus' transcendent status. But did not still earlier factors, perhaps including Jesus' self-awareness, already contribute to the shaping of this slumbering conviction? In conceding this latter possibility Moule goes beyond Pannenberg's insistence that: "Until his resurrection, Jesus' unity with God was hidden not only to other men but above all, which emerges from a critical examination of the tradition, for Jesus himself also. It was hidden because the ultimate decision about it had not been given" (1977:321). Moule to the contrary stresses that the New Testament writings share a common "devotion to the person of Jesus Christ, the historical Jesus acknowledged as Messiah and Lord" (1966:9), a veneration that did not first emerge after Jesus' resurrection (cf. Luke 24:21).

Moule (1966:140-41) does not specifically address the question of Jesus' virgin birth, stating only that "even . . . at its most reduced level . . . [of] . . . myth, one might still maintain that it was an expression of that transcendental quality which, from the very beginning, seems to have attached to Christ. . . ." But in that case might not Christ's preexistence, empty tomb, resurrection, and ascension ministry be assimilated similarly to this reductionist level? Moule's declaration that the canonical writings need not as such be regarded as wholly trustworthy (1966:136-37) serves only to widen doubts about historical factuality. It is not enough to reject as inadequate, as Moule indeed does, J. L. Houlden's view that the new life that early Christians found in Jesus, and their consequent experience of a new world, constrained them to view Jesus as the preexistent agent of its creation (1975:103-05). To reinforce Houlden's view only by Moule's emphasis that the first Christians "experienced Jesus himself as in a dimension transcending the human and the temporal" (1977:138) insufficiently illumines the transcendent basis of that experience and the validity-claim attaching to it. The earliest Christians, Moule avers, were "driven to their conclusions by the force of what was happening to them" (1977:162). Yet this appeal to the implications of apostolic experience for the transcendent nature of Christ is vulnerable through Moule's failure to elaborate an adequate revelation-grounded theology of the person and work of the Redeemer.

Reginald Fuller finds in the historical Jesus more than an expressed basis for the apostolic *Kerygma*. He emphasizes that there exists "a direct line of continuity between Jesus' self-understanding and the church's christological interpretation of him" (1965:15,108,254). "Jesus understood his mission in terms of eschatological prophecy" and as actually initiating in his own words and works the expected future salvation and judgment. "Take the implied self-understanding of his role in terms of the eschatological prophet away, and the whole ministry falls into a series of unrelated, if not meaningless, fragments" (1965:130).

Yet Fuller contends that Jesus never publicly proclaimed himself the Messiah, nor did he impose a christology on his disciples (1954:116). When Peter identified him as Messiah, Jesus charged his disciples not to broadcast the news but began to speak of his impending suffering (Mark 8:29-31). Only at the end when, condemned to die as a messianic pretender, he was asked if he were the Messiah and when he was about to be crucified, he answered "I am" or "Yes, it is as you say" (Mark 15:2, cf. 15:9, 26).

Peter Stuhlmacher (1988) insists that the explicit post-Easter christology of the Early Church is grounded in Jesus' pre-Easter self-understanding. He declares wholly unacceptable the alternative that the *Kerygma* is essentially a human product, as Bultmann and post-Bultmannians held. To ground Jesus' deity upon the faith of believers is to rest the claims of Christianity on interpretation rather than on historical actuality and substitutes superstition for truth. The high Christology, says J. L. M. Haire, "is in the words of Jesus Himself, in His 'But I say unto you,' His knowledge of the Father, and His victory over the powers of evil" (1956:96).

Where it suits their purposes, mediating writers often secretly rely on a conservative rather than a critical view of the biblical accounts. And yet it is not only conservatives like R. T. France, who consider it "probable that some, and perhaps all, of the Gospels were written in substantially their present form within thirty years of the events, and that much of the material was already collected and written a decade or two before that" (1986). For France's view of early sources is here not dissimilar from that of the critical and quite radical New Testament scholar John A. T. Robinson, except for France's avoidance of Robinson's vulnerable dating method. Thus, the Gospels serve as substantial and trustworthy testimonies to Jesus.

The Significance of Miracles

Once the question of historical facticity of the Gospels is raised earnestly, the subject of miracles is unavoidable. Not only do the Gospels attribute remarkable miracles to Jesus before his death and resurrection, but they also assign to these acts a role and importance that distinguish Jesus from other miracle-workers. As Colin Brown (1985) emphasizes, the miracles fulfilled John the Baptist's prophecy of the Messiah's coming in demonstration of the Spirit. The Hebrew religious hierarchy, by contrast, saw the miracles as wonders that detoured the masses from orthodoxy and in view of this called for the destruction of Jesus.

G. F. Woods thinks a high degree of probability attaches to claims for the resurrection and many New Testament miracles (1965:21). Yet he emphasizes that what seems beyond human power is not axiomatically divine. Our secular technocratic age notably dwarfs the evidential value of miracles. Even if we could show that some events are not human, it does not necessarily follow that they are supernatural. But it should be emphasized also that one will consider no event whatever truly miraculous if he disbelieves in the supernatural. A philosophical naturalist would insist not simply that miracles have ceased in post-biblical times, but that they have never occurred. Even if he were present at the Second Coming of Christ, he might at first insist that he was the victim of a cosmic illusion or afflicted by a brain tumor. The notion that the biblical writers believed in miracles because as pre-scientific men they were ignorant of the laws of nature is preposterous. One is tempted to say they knew enough biology and physics to know that the virgin birth and the resurrection of Jesus were once-for-all historical acts.

But that way of putting it would only sustain the misconception that observational science can identify once-for-all events, whereas in fact it is impotent to do so. For all science knows, there may have been or may still be other virgin births and resurrections. Science in the future may even simulate biblical happenings, but such simulation would have no bearing on what occurred in Bethlehem and Jerusalem ca. A.D. 30. It is knowledge of God and his purposes rather than ignorance of science and its inferences and assumptions that explains the scriptural insistence on the miraculous in biblical history.

The New Testament does not permit us to see the universe either as a closed mechanical system of unbroken regularity or as an open haphazard chaos of only contrived predictability, or of capricious determinations by mythical divinities. The Christian theist holds that the sense of the universe is to be found in the purposive revelation of God who is personally sovereign and free in sustaining both cosmic continuities and unique once-for-all events.

One of the church fathers, Athanasius, author of *On the Incarnation*, suggests the cosmic Christ became incarnate so that those who did not recognize his works in nature would acknowledge him through his works done in the flesh. As C. S. Lewis puts it, "the Christian story is precisely the story of one grand miracle, the Christian assertion being that what is beyond all space and time, what is uncreated, eternal, came into nature, into human nature, descended into his own universe and rose again, bringing nature up with him" (1970:80).

Indeed, Jesus is himself the Miracle—the One who binds Satan and releases the penitent from Satan's grip. If one accepts the reality of divine incarnation in Jesus Christ, the possibility of miracles is implicit in the Great Miracle; as Colin Hemer comments, it is "a natural corollary of that *Weltanschauung*" (1989:442). The Enlightenment hostility to miracles, he adds, arose not from "freedom from presupposition," but from contrary presupposition (ibid., 443).

The central thesis of the Gospel of John is that Jesus' works are signs of the nearing fulfillment of the Old Testament prophecies of redemption and that they manifest Jesus as the Christ, the Son of God. The raising of Lazarus after his death and burial serves notice that Jesus has life-giving power beyond death and is a foregleam of the coming general resurrection in which Jews believed.

Yet for all that, the Gospel of Luke makes abundantly clear that the disciples did not grasp Jesus' predictions of his own third-day resurrection. In those resurrection appearances Jesus made unmistakable connections with his precrucifixion ministry (cf. Henry, 1979:3:159-60). The resurrection is not to be wholly detached from the contribution of Jesus' preresurrection teaching and works to his designation as Lord.

The first Christians, as Hodgson says in a preface for the paperback edition of his Gifford Lectures, were "Palestinian Jews trying to fit their faith in the risen Lord into their inherited Jewish theology" (1968:1:xi). Yet their inherited religion supplied prophetic intimations and anticipations of the exceptional role and nature of Messiah whose coming was divinely pledged. The fact that some modern interpreters have read back into the Old Testament christological intentions and meanings that seem foreign to it is no reason for minimizing the extensive basis which the New Testament writers, and not least of all the authors of the Gospels, found in the Old Testament for accrediting Jesus of Nazareth as the Christ. The Old Testament nurtured expectation of the coming 'Son of David' born in the Davidic line, the Suffering Servant, the supernatural 'Son of Man,' and the transcendent intervention of God to establish his Kingdom. "Christian faith began," Hodgson notes, "with the acceptance of his claim to be the fulfillment of God's messianic promises given through the Old Testament prophets. Had there been no previous history of Israel, there would have been...no New Testament" (1968:82).

The Resurrection and Divinity

The resurrection of the crucified Jesus holds in Christianity a pivotal importance for the affirmation of Jesus' divinity. Bultmann scorned all talk of an empty tomb or of the crucified Nazarene's bodily appearances; the only resurrection he allowed occurred not in Jerusalem, but in the believer's internal response to the preaching of the apostles. The beginnings of christology for Bultmann therefore lay not in any historical ontological happening on "the third day" but in an existential event whose character is functional. "Whether one argues that Christology began within the consciousness of Jesus, or later somewhere within the life and faith of the early Christian community," Berkey comments, "the substance of Christology is always shaped by, created by, understood through the New Testament's resounding affirmation, 'He is risen!'" (1982:18).

Moule is surely right that Christianity does not rest solely or merely on "certain antecedent claims made by or for Jesus...but rather on the implications of his life, his actions, his teaching, his death, and most notably its extraordinary sequel" (1977:163). The Easter verdict seems to Moule decisive because he finds it "impossible to account for...except as an intimation traceable only to Christ himself" (1977:173) and because subsequent history supplies no evidence for reversing that verdict. Can historical investigation alone, however, provide a solid basis for an irreversible verdict on the permanent aliveness of Jesus Christ? Granted that a conclusively negative verdict on the factual resurrection of the crucified Jesus would devastate Christian faith, the question remains whether empirical historical inquiry can decisively adjudicate the question of Jesus' present aliveness and high priestly ministry.

It is not to historiography—"new" or old—that we look for validation of Jesus' claim to reveal God, but only for verification that he made such a claim and worked certain acts and lived in a certain way and said certain things that seem quite inconsistent logically with any other claim. When Van Harvey tells us that "there is no *one true* significance of an event" (cited by Moule, 1977:221) he arbitrarily presumes to tell us that the importance of the life and death of Jesus is not to be identified in terms of a divinely revealed meaning, and hence that the attribution of such significance to it is untrue.

Is the resurrection to be seen as a confirmation of Jesus' divine teaching and work, or is it rather the event in which christology took its rise? Michael Walsh (1986) resurrects the modernist thesis that Jesus' victory over death was a matter of faith more than a historical fact: "all that really matters is that those who followed Jesus believed the resurrection to have taken place and they acted on that belief." W. H. C. Frend argues that only because Jesus was already accepted as unique could the Easter story have gained currency (1984:55). Surely something about Jesus' life and ministry contributed to the credibility of the resurrection reports. But the Gospels in no way support a theory that the resurrection is grounded in the disciples' psychological condition.

Peter Carnley (1987) asserts that New Testament faith in the resurrection was grounded in an encounter exempt from rational inquiry into the basis of belief. Carnley stresses the post-crucifixion role of the phenomena of "appearance" and "presence," the former only to believers (or in Paul's case to one acquainted with Jesus), and yet sufficiently ambiguous, Carnley thinks, to allow doubt. Yet the experience is not merely private, but also "communal and publicly shared." The Holy Spirit's presence, Carnley contends, is a presence of Jesus Christ. Carnley's treatment lacks a careful statement of the particular roles of appearance, of experience, and of liturgical remembrance in assuring the reality of the resurrection of the Crucified One; and he does not work out implications of the pre-Easter ministry of Jesus contributing to this assurance.

Among current literature that goes behind psychology to a larger historical rootedness for Jesus' message and mission—although not necessarily to adequate discussion of the words of Jesus—are E. P. Sanders's *Jesus and the Spiral of Violence* (1987), and Marcus J. Borg's *Jesus: A New Vision* (1987). These works, as Borg himself comments, halt short of both direct quotation by and specific attribution to Jesus, do not argue for historical exactitude in details, and are especially interested in socio-cultural implications (1988:280-92).

The case for the objective historical resurrection of the crucified Jesus has been maintained not by evangelical orthodox scholars alone, but by others also who emphasize both the empty tomb and Jesus' resurrection appearances. Wolfhart Pannenberg (1968) considers Jesus' resurrection decisive for every christological concern. He does so, however, in a controversial way: in his view, the earthly life of Jesus is "kenosis"—a condition in which his divinity was imperceptible and in which his fellow-Jews could only regard him as a blasphemer. Pannenberg speaks of "Jesus' nonmessianic ministry" as being "*transformed* into Christology only in the light of the resurrection," and insists, as Berkey notes, that what "divides the nonmessianic historical Jesus from the Christ of faith is not an affirmation but an event" (1982:20). The resurrection he considers a real, external, nonexistential historical event, not a mythical existential reinterpretation. Yet in doing so he also sacrifices a Logos-theology. Contrary to Barth, Lawson, Moule, Guthrie, and others, he develops christology "from below." He rules out the virgin birth as legend and derives from the Early Church the titles that the Gospels ascribe to Jesus. Divine authority was merely "implicit" in Jesus' three-year ministry; only the resurrection vindicates it. The resurrection thus displaces the incarnation as the starting-point for the discussion of Jesus' deity (cf. E. Frank Tupper, 1971).

Yet Pannenberg denies revelation in the form of scriptural prophecy and insists instead that revelation is given in self-interpreting history. He critically rejects the unity of Scripture, forfeits canonical inspiration, defers to noncanonical materials, and professes to find the meaning of history in history itself, rather than in Scripture. While he contends for a unified history centered in the figure of Jesus, his critically concessive view of the Gospels leads him to depict Jesus as mistakenly expecting an imminent end of world history and leads him also to deny that Jesus portrayed himself as the coming Son of man. Instead of appealing to divinely authoritative and historically reliable Scripture, he insists that Jesus' resurrection "is not made certain by faith but only by historical research" and then adds the significant qualifier, "to the extent that certainty can be attained at all about questions of this kind" (cited by Tupper, 1971:99).

But history is in fact not self-interpreting, nor is empirical historical investigation capable of yielding more than high probability. Inspired Scripture speaks prophetically of the resurrection of the Crucified One. Jesus' disciples at first heeded neither the biblical intimations nor their Master's anticipations of that event. Yet the apostle Paul gave Jesus' resurrection due centrality (1 Cor. 15:3-4), insisting both on its scriptural prediction and its historical factuality.

Although radical form-criticism and redaction criticism shroud the Gospels in historical uncertainty, archaeological discovery continues its sporadic confirmation even of the Bible's obscure details. Nonetheless, Pannenberg attaches little more theological significance to Jesus' messianic consciousness and words and deeds than do most post-Bultmannian scholars. The tradition of the resurrection appearances and that of the empty tomb, he holds, arose independently. Yet their complementarity makes Jesus' historical resurrection "very probable and that always means in historical inquiry that it is to be presupposed until contrary evidence appears" (ibid., 105); certainty will not come until there is eschatological verification. But is it enough to say that apostolic Christianity proclaimed the resurrection of Jesus Christ merely as highly probable?

John Cobb, who accepts the historical probability of the resurrection, considers the empty tomb reports cognitively more vulnerable than the appearances (1969:199-200). At the same time he finds confirmation of the tradition of Jesus' appearances in present-day visionary "appearances" of the dead, a comparison that wholly misses the theological and eschatological significance of Jesus' resurrection. Cobb emphasizes that Jesus' appearances lack features usually associated with a body, but thinks the differences are minimized by focusing on one's post-mortem spiritual life rather than on the nature of bodily resurrection. Speculative considerations here override the importance of an authentic New Testament witness.

Pannenberg affirms the resurrection not only to be decisive for the recognition of Jesus' divinity, but also as ontologically constitutive of the reality of his divinity. Therefore, it is remarkable that he seems in the face of rival theological and exegetical expositions increasingly to shy away from Jesus' resurrection as an historical event (cf. Gerald O'Collins, 1968) or at least to consider all approaches to Jesus' resurrection to be merely provisional. He insists, on the one hand, that if the resurrection claim is valid it is so as an historical act in the past. Yet, on the other hand, he declares it "quite difficult to affirm this event as a fact in the same sense as other facts...I presuppose that history does not require homogeneity of all events which are designated as historical" (cited by Tupper, 1971:284-85).

Many conservatives initially hailed Pannenberg for his rejection of neo-orthodox fideism and for his insistence on divine revelation in history, and the importance of histori- cally attested divine acts as indispensable to the Christian faith. These revelatory acts reached their climax in the history of Jesus consummated by his resurrection, attesting Jesus' divinity, emphasized particularly in the empty tomb accounts and the Pauline report of the resurrection appear- ances. Pannenberg questions Willi Marxsen's view that the Easter witnesses claim only to have seen Jesus who was crucified, and not to have seen him rise (because admittedly there were no human eyewitnesses of the resurrection *event* per se). Their reflective interpretation, says Marxsen (1968:30-31), was that God raised Jesus. Marxsen's approach could in principle divorce the appearances from any linkage whatever to Jesus. Pannenberg concedes that only in the eschatological end-time will we speak clearly about what happened in Jesus' resurrection. The revelation God gives in the risen Jesus is *proleptic*—i.e., an advance disclosure in Jesus the individual of a comprehensive end-time consummation; more- over, it is paradoxical and metaphorical, in short, doxological, and not given in the form of universally valid truth (1977:187, 397). Pannenberg holds that "the appearances reported in the Gospels, which are not mentioned by Paul, have such a strong legendary character that no one can scarcely find a historical kernel of their own in them (1977:107)." Such radical criticism cannot but reflect negatively on claims for Jesus' resurrection.

According to Pannenberg, Jesus' resurrection must be veri- fiable in principle by historical reason independently of faith. Jurgen Moltmann (1967:82) counters that such historical verification would require a concept of history that would anticipate the prophesied end of history, one dominated by an expectation of universal endtime resurrection (1967:82). Pannenberg has modified his view to hold that in history we have only "pointers" to the resurrection and that the resurrection of Jesus will "possess and retain the character of revelation for us" (1977:107). But, as Avery Dulles comments, if divine promise is, as Pannenberg implies, "only the anticipation of revelation," and if "at the moment that Jesus becomes the fulfillment of the promise he passes beyond the limits of history," it would seem that as long as history lasts we are doomed to be deprived of revelation itself (1985:65).

The Jewish New Testament scholar Pinchas Lapide (1984) grants that the crucified Jesus arose from the dead. No other explanation, such as vision or hallucination, he says, can explain the revolutionary transformation of Jesus' disciples after Easter weekend. Although Lapide concedes the material facticity of Jesus' resurrection, he dismisses as pious fraud such narrative details in the Gospel accounts as the disciples' discovery of the empty tomb and the appearance of angelic creatures in white garments. He asserts that the resurrection experience helped advance the divine plan of salvation and declares that Jesus could be the Messiah of the Gentiles. Yet he denies that Jesus was the long-awaited Jewish messiah or divine Son of God.

The ground and hope common to the Old and New Testaments, however, precludes any such distinction. Messiah is Savior of the world, not simply of Jews and of Gentiles, and his third-day resurrection attests his messiahship in the context of the biblical hope and prospect of a final resurrection of all mankind.

Historical research by itself is incompetent to establish the New Testament's most significant statements about Jesus Christ. It may indeed attest that Jesus lived and died in Palestine and that he "taught with authority." But it cannot confirm that he was conceived by the Holy Spirit, or that he is the eternal Logos become flesh and veritable divine Son through whom God has ushered in the last days, or that he arose from the dead never to die again, or that God has made him both Lord and Christ, or that he will return in omnipotent power and glory.

3

The Larger Biblical Witness to Jesus

Old Testament and New Testament

Earlier generations appealed more eagerly than ours to the predictive content of the Old Testament. Modernism with its denial of the miraculous and dialectical and existential theology with its insistence on the uniformity of nature and its internalization of miracle, disavowed predictive prophecy.

The first Christians were, as Hodgson (1968:1:xi) says in a preface for the paperback edition of his Gifford Lectures, "Palestinian Jews trying to fit their faith in the risen Lord into their inherited Jewish theology." Yet their inherited religion had itself supplied prophetic intimations and anticipations of the exceptional role and nature of Messiah whose coming was divinely pledged. The fact that some modern interpreters have read back into the Old Testament christological intentions and meanings that seem foreign to it is no reason for minimizing the extensive basis which the New Testament writers, and not least of all the authors of the Gospels, found in the Old Testament for accrediting Jesus of Nazareth as the Christ. "Christian faith began," Hodgson notes, "with the acceptance of his claim to be the fulfillment of God's messianic promises given through the Old Testament prophets. Had there been no previous history of Israel, there would have been ... no New Testament" (1:82).

The evasion of supernatural prediction is reflected in Claus Westermann's treatment of "The Psalms and Christ" in which he sets aside messianic prophecy for what he describes as "a more profound and comprehensive" Old Testament anchoring of the Christ-event (1980:27). But if God cannot foretell the future in specifics, can he prefigure them in generalities? The writers of the Gospels and of the Epistles unhesitatingly appealed to the Old Testament predictions of the coming Messiah.

Although Jewish and Gentile sources both supplied linguistic factors for the early Church's identification of Jesus as God-man, the Christian doctrine of Jesus Christ did not spring from a simple borrowing of existing Hebrew or Greek semantic elements. Jesus' own teaching and life impacted notably and transformingly upon Logos and Wisdom theology. Christianity's ties to Judaism, moreover, are firmer than the links that comparative religions scholars often postulate between Christianity and Greek thought. Discovery of the Dead Sea Scrolls encouraged new investigation of Old Testament backgrounds, rather than of Gentile religion or philosophy as the context illuminating New Testament thought. W. D. Davies (1948, 1967) had emphasized already a generation ago that the religious background of Pauline theology is Judaic rather than Hellenistic. Recent New Testament scholarship has looked more to the Jewish and less to the Gentile religious milieu to illumine christological titles such as Lord and Son of God. This verdict, that New Testament christology has roots in the Old Testament rather than in Graeco-Roman philosophy and religion, is immensely important. Yet Christian belief in the divinity of Jesus Christ turned even more decisively on the events and teachings of the Gospels than on pre-Christian considerations.

We cannot, of course, gloss over highly conflicting perceptions regarding the Gospel writings. Bultmann declared the Gospel tradition historically unreliable. He made the early Church's creative imagination decisive for christology; the kerygma is confirmed not by historical data but by resurrection-faith. Thus Bultmann wholly severed christology from Jesus' self-understanding, from his self-disclosure, from the testimony of eyewitnesses, from a carefully controlled oral tradition, and from any reliable narrative of Jesus' life and teaching.

Contrary to Bultmann's insistence that John 20:28 ("my Lord and my God") is the only New Testament passage to designate Jesus as God (1955:276), Raymond E. Brown stipulates "three clear instances" (John 1:1; 20:28; Heb. 1:8) and five probable instances. The post-apostolic designation of

Jesus as *theos* (God), Brown declares, is therefore "a continuation of a usage already begun in New Testament times" (1967:28-29). Brown recognizes that the affirmation by Thomas is "strongly confessional and existential," and that "most of the other instances" are liturgical or confessional. Bultmann would take any and all such statements not as dogmatic descriptions or objectifying statements but rather as declarations of personal significance: "The formula, 'Christ is God,'" he contended, "is false in every sense in which God can be understood as an entity which can be objectivized" (1955:287).

Yet an unbiased reader can hardly avoid the New Testament's ontological claims for Jesus. Some leading Scandinavian, British, and American New Testament scholars pointedly reject a form-critical approach and disavow even more especially the philosophical assumptions to which Bultmann welded it. The Swiss scholar Oscar Cullmann vigorously assailed Bultmann's form-critical method and rejected existential philosophy as tendential and destructive.

Many Swedish scholars insist that the Gospel writers preserve a professional oral tradition, while Anglo-American scholars emphasize that the New Testament need not be considered creative myth simply because it reflects the views of the early Church. The prime issue is whether claims for Jesus made by the first-century Church represent a fundamental break in the way Jesus' disciples conceived of him and in the way Jesus their teacher conceived of himself. The early Church's christological outlook no doubt discloses a development. But is there, for all that, an essential continuity between its preresurrection and postresurrection beliefs and representations?

The Christological Titles

C. F. D. Moule (1977) contends that the substance of the main christological titles—Son of man, Son of God, Christ, the Lord—is present already in the very thought and teaching of Jesus, and moreover, that his claims are not merely functional but ontological. I. Howard Marshall (1976) similarly locates Christology within Jesus' self-affirmation. Martin Hengel (1976) too rejects the notion that the early Church's christology breaks decisively with Jesus' own claims. The preresurrection message of Jesus, he holds, provided indispensable struts for the Christology of the early Church. Despite the vigorous counterclaims of Bultmannian and post-Bultmannian critics, many scholars share this emphasis that Christology begins with Jesus of Nazareth. The Synoptic titles thus stand impressively linked to the "I am" declarations of the Gospel of John.

Jesus' self-testimony is best considered under two aspects, the names or titles he applied to himself, and his references to his own person.

The titles Son of David, Son of God, and Messiah were used of Jesus by others, but not used by Jesus of himself. Most widely used of the titles are the Son-of-man sayings which bear importantly on Jesus' messianic self-consciousness. This title is, Berkey says, "the only presumed messianic designation that the synoptic writers have placed directly on the lips of Jesus" as used by him in the third person. Moreover, in Mark 14:62, Jesus indirectly applied the title to himself in the context of an express claim to be the Messiah. To be sure, P. Vielhauer considers all the titles inauthentic, and Bultmann regards them as sheer inventions of the early church. But the Gospel Evangelists indicate that, as Cullmann (1959) emphasizes, Jesus wished to be understood as "Son of man."

Bultmann conceded that Jesus used this title. But he held that Jesus referred it not to himself but to an apocalyptic figure; the early Church only later, Bultmann contended, identified this figure with the resurrected Jesus. More recent redaction critics widen the gap between Jesus' proclamation and the later Church's christological claims by removing each and every Son of man saying from the earliest layers of authentic Jesus-tradition. But the Gospels depict Jesus being tried and sentenced not only for calling God his Father (John 5:18) but also for his usage of the title "Son of Man."

Barnabas Lindars in *Jesus—Son of Man* (1983:158) insists that Daniel 7:13 has a collective or community sense and dismisses the claim that Jewish messianism used the term as the title of an eschatological figure. Lindars holds that the Gospel writers subsequently applied the title to Jesus. But if so, the absence of a Son-of-Man christology in the remainder of the New Testament is difficult to explain. Slim though the evidence may be, there is some support for Jewish use of the title for an apocalyptic figure, but no conclusive basis for the theory that the church independently imposed the term on the Nazarene.

F. F. Bruce (1982:50) stresses, however, that in Jesus' day "the Son of man" was not a current title "for the Messiah or any other eschatological figure." Jesus' use was derived, he holds, from the reference in Daniel 7:13 to "one like a 'son of man'...divinely vested with authority." Jesus fused this title with the figure of a suffering servant—"probably the Isaianic Servant." Bruce concludes that "a 'Son of man' theology could be nothing other than a theology based on what can be ascertained about Jesus' understanding of his identity and life-mission." Likewise Martin Hengel (1976) connects the idea of divine sonship with Jesus' own proclamation and traces to Jesus himself the affirmation of his divine incarnation and vicarious atonement. In contrast to H. J. Schoeps (1961:158) and other *Religionsgeschichte* partisans who declare "the 'Son of God' belief to be the sole, albeit decisive, heathen premise of Pauline thought," Hengel insists the title can be understood only on Jewish assumptions (cf. W. R. Long, 1989:232). A. J. B. Higgins (1981) insists that Jesus expected a vindication of his ministry by exaltation that included "judgmental functions traditionally associated with the apocalyptic Son of Man."

Bultmann had rejected—appropriately enough, but not for good reason—the modernist appeal to a non-miraculous historical Jesus behind the *Kerygma*. But he then lifted the Gospel texts from an historical setting and turned them into speculative abstraction. Post-Bultmannians sought to narrow the gap between the preached Christ and the historical Jesus. But their form-critical method continued to limit the objective factuality of the Gospels, and moreover they had no interest in probing Jesus' messianic awareness. The beginnings of Christology, in their view, lies not in claims made by the Jesus of history or in the pre-Easter proclamations of disciples influenced by his life and teaching, but essentially in the early Church as a post-Easter community of faith.

Marcus J. Borg (1987) depicts Jesus as "a Spirit-filled," charismatically-motivated person who regarded himself as prophet and may have thought of himself as the Son of God, but did not publicly proclaim himself to be such. Much the same verdict is given by Ragnar Leivestad (1987) and by James H. Charlesworth (1988).

There is growing acknowledgment of the need to move beyond the many contradictory critical discussions of Christology to a reexamination of the New Testament documents. If contemporary Gospel studies reflect any trend, it is a resurgent interest in the Jesus of history, including larger attention to Jesus' message and works. C. F. D. Moule notes the "unexamined false assumptions behind a good deal of contemporary New Testament scholarship." Moule specially faults the notion that "the genesis of Christology...can be explained as a sort of evolutionary process" whereby what began with a view of Jesus as a Palestinian rabbi evolved gradually into the affirmation of "the divine Lord of a Hellenistic Saviour-cult" (1977:1-2).

Moule readily grants a "development" in New Testament Christology. But he insists that this unfolding articulates and refines what Jesus and his followers had affirmed from the outset. With an eye on the Aramaic term *marana tha*, found in the earliest Pauline literature (1 Cor 16:22), Moule comments that one does not "call upon a dead rabbi to come" (1973:562-65). The term in fact echoes the longing of the community of believers for the Lord's glorious return. Moule stresses that, as the Qumran scrolls attest, the Semitic term *mar* ("Master") was used not simply of a rabbi or human master but of God or gods also. In speaking of Jesus, moreover, monotheistic Jews who spoke Greek employed not simply the term *Kurios* current in the Greek world of their day but even and especially *Kurios*-passages from the Septuagint translation of the Old Testament. Reginald Fuller (1965:119) notes that Jesus had prepared the way for the highest sense of *mar* when during his earthly ministry he asked, "Why do you call me 'Lord, Lord' and not do what I tell you?"

This assertion of an apostolic continuity with Jesus' own christological claims Moule bases not mainly on Jesus' words but more broadly on evidence that "from very early days, Jesus was being interpreted as an inclusive Israel-wide—indeed, Adam-wide—person: one who, as no merely human individual, included persons and communities within him, and upon whom Christians found converging all the patterns of relationship between God and man with which they were familiar from their Scriptures" (1977:136). Jesus was held obediently to fulfill the divinely given vocation in which Israel had failed. Even New Testament writers who are not explicit about the larger ontological implications nonetheless assign Jesus "more than individual implications" in their "conceptions of him as the convergence-point of all the Old Testament patterns of relationship between God and his people, and as the universal Saviour," says Moule; moreover, "Paul's understanding of Jesus is like a theist's understanding of God—that he is personal but more than individual," and even in those parts of the New Testament where Christ is conceived of much more individualistically, he is nevertheless conceived of as "definitely transcendent and divine" (1977:138).

"Jesus is certainly called God within the New Testament (John 20:28 and probably Tit 2:13)," Moule emphasizes (1977:137). Bruce M. Metzger (1973:109) holds, moreover, that Jesus was expressly being called "God" as early as the Pauline letters, a circumstance that would demolish the notion that the ascription of divinity reflects a non-Jewish borrowing from pagan sources.

The person of Jesus himself, Moule contends, is one way or another the source of the remarkable estimates of him as 'the Son of Man,' 'the Son of God,' 'Messiah,' and 'Kurios.'

From an analysis of the titles of Jesus found already in the Gospel of Mark (especially Son of Man, Lord, Christ, Son of David, Son of God), Ferdinand Hahn (1963; 1969) argues that a hellenistic Jewish Christianity existed alongside a Palestinian Jewish Christianity and a pre-Pauline hellenistic Christianity. This accommodates a smoother link between Palestinian Jewish and hellenistic Jewish and hellenistic Christian belief, and implies a direct continuity between Jesus and the New Testament Christology.

Donald Guthrie (1981) expounds New Testament Christology on the premise that Jesus' divinity is a biblically given datum guaranteed by divine revelation. His appeal to Scripture as decisive for the doctrine of Christ has the clear advantage of escaping constantly changing alternatives reflecting novel metaphysical principles or extra-canonical post-apostolic documents. But it does not of itself assure interpretations of the biblical data on scripture's own terms. The appeal to the New Testament was made, for example, by advocates of a "kenotic" Christology and by proponents of a "moral union" Christology, both of which compromised the deity of Jesus Christ through their imposition of tendential assumptions on the scriptural data.

Karl Rahner holds that the "titles of dignity" reflect Jesus' own belief in the Johnnanine and Pauline teaching of the doctrine of divine preexistence of the Son-Logos and his claim to have been divinely sent. But he contends that the New Testament goes beyond Jesus' witness to himself (1974:4:492). The Judeo-Hellenistic doctrine of a wisdom anterior to the world, he holds, would have led to faith in Jesus' preexistence and hence the affirmation of a divine incarnation (1974:4:194). But then, as Joseph Siri (1980) indicates, the inference is difficult to avoid that Nicea and Chalcedon crystallized a post-resurrection affirmation that Jesus is God incarnate, a view presumably not held earlier either by the Evangelists before the resurrection or found in the self-consciousness or self-revelation of Jesus of Nazareth during his three year ministry. The implication is that ascending theological speculation transformed headlong a more primitive view of Jesus into the doctrine of the incarnation of a preexistent Word-Son.

More recently James D. G. Dunn (1980) presumes to find a variety of christological views in the New Testament and regards the preexistent Logos subsequently incarnate in Christ as but one of these options. To be sure, Dunn shows that the Christian doctrine of Christ's incarnation was not dependent upon a Gnostic redeemer myth, contrary to some skeptics. He concedes that as a feature of the Fourth Gospel, John 1:14 in affirming the incarnation of the pre-existent Logos-Son, sponsors a fully personal doctrine of the divine preexistence of Jesus Christ. Even in the text of John 1:1-13, however, Dunn finds not an emphasis on the Logos' personal preexistence, but rather only a personified utterance of God.

Dunn needlessly sacrifices other substantial supports of

New Testament Christology. He finds no explicit doctrine of the incarnation in the Pauline writings and contends moreover that not even Hebrews offers a fully personal doctrine of preexistence. He writes: "Only in the post-Pauline period did a clear understanding of Christ as having preexisted with God before his ministry on earth emerge, and only in the Fourth Gospel can we speak of a doctrine of the incarnation" (1980:259).

But G. B. Caird affirms the preexistence doctrine to be an intrinsic feature of Pauline Christology (1968:68-71.). C. F. D. Moule (1982) points out, moreover, that Dunn's sweeping dismissal of the Pauline corpus rests on questionable exegesis of such passages as Phil 2:5ff. and Col 1:15ff. The New Testament affirms more than that Jesus Christ embodies and discloses the nature of the invisible creative powers and the spirit of love that sustains the world. Dunn's emphasis that the Pauline letters refer only to Jesus' post-resurrection status and contain no intimation of Christ's ontological preexistence and incarnation, and that even Hebrews affirms preexistence only as a conceptual idea rather than as actual personal preexistence, rests on biased aprioris in reading passages like Rom 8:3; Gal 4:4; and Phil 2:6-7, and Heb 1:2-3; 2:6-9; and 7:3.

L. William Countryman (1982:335) protests likewise that Dunn's argument rests on weak and highly vulnerable assumptions. Dunn contends, for example, that the several New Testament christological titles (Son of man, new Adam, Son of God, etc.) depict distinct christologies, and that terms like Logos and Wisdom can mean only what pre-Christian writers meant by them. In these circumstances Dunn overlooks the possibility that christological titles may to some extent have been used interchangeably , and that Logos and Wisdom in the New Testament have significant personal overtones. What Dunn considers central in New Testament Christology, Countryman adds, he expresses in language that is incompatible with the biblical texts (1982, p. 335).

While there is a developing Christology in the New Testament, Dunn's exposition of a gradually emerging incarnational view prejudicially assigns the stimulus for incarnational theology not to apostolic revelation or to Jesus' knowledge of himself, but rather to enlarging Christian faith. The notion that in its early stages the exaltation of Jesus was distinct from belief in his divine preexistence (1980:63, 162-63) seems moreover to jeopardize the monotheism on which the New Testament everywhere insists.

Donald Guthrie responds to the recent tendency, especially among redaction critics, to find in the New Testament not an integrated theological perspective but rather a reflection of supposedly diverse views of the several biblical writers. Guthrie counters that the New Testament writers do not expound independent creative theologies: the corpus does not contain "a collection of different theologies rather than...a unified New Testament theology" (1981:71). The unprejudiced interpreter "is not at liberty to pick and choose" from the New Testament data, Guthrie cautions, in order to conform its representations to preconceived theories.

Cullmann holds that the early Christian christological formulations articulate what is already presupposed in the earliest literature about Jesus. But while Cullmann insists that "christology already underlies the New Testament," he holds that Christology is less interested in the *nature* of Jesus than in his function. He stresses that the New Testament answers the question of the *function* of Jesus not in terms of myth but in terms of "actual events...that involve his life, work, death and presence and actions after his crucifixion" (1959:316).

Reginald Fuller complains that Cullmann's disposition to view New Testament Christology as almost exclusively functional disregards the latest stratum of the biblical literature, and lacks continuity with the still later patristic contribution (1965:247, 257). Philippians 2, for example, is no less expressly ontological than is John 1 and should not be taken as merely the translation into Greek of earlier asserted functional activities.

To affirm Christ's personal divine preexistence is simultaneously to deny that Jesus Christ is a man who gradually became God. Although Jesus' contemporaries, even his disciples, may only gradually have perceived the deity of the God-man, he was not, for all that, a devout human being who acquired divinity in the course of spiritual development, or, was he, as

D. M. Baillie adds, God or the Son of God "transformed into a human being for a period of about thirty years" (1948:82). New Testament Christianity depicts Jesus as at one and the same time both God and man.

Nothing in the Gospels indicates that Jesus arrogantly or ostentatiously displayed his deity or overwhelmed even his closest disciples by it. Yet John's Gospel records his magisterial *I am*s as overt claims. Guthrie comments that "it is difficult to escape the conclusion that in the mind of Jesus there was a connection with the great *I AM* as the name of Jehovah" in the Old Testament, particularly in view of John 8:58 (1975, vol. 3, p. 569). An implicit Christology lies in the tender term *abba* (cf. J. Jeremias, 1965:9-10) and in the insistence on his unique sonship (cf. Matt. 11:25-30), which imply that the Father and the Son share the same essential life. The conjunction of Jesus' name with that of both the Father and the Spirit supports this. His divine prerogatives, as his life and teaching make clear, include the forgiveness of sins in his own name, and the future judgment as well of all humanity.

Worship of the Risen Lord

In recognizing Jesus as the promised Messiah, his disciples subscribed to Jesus' own belief about himself, even if they only glimpsed some aspects of all that messianity meant to him. It was not worship uninformed by cognitive considerations that motivated the disciples' attitude toward Jesus. D. A. Carson thinks it premature "to minimize the Christological implications of Jesus' historical self-disclosure" (1982:97-126). He finds many subtle claims of Jesus to deity in Matthew's Gospel alone even if full understanding awaited the resurrection (1982:110). In his quotation of Psalm 110 in which the Messiah is not only the Son of David but also David's 'Lord,' Jesus applied this title to himself (Matt 22:41-46). Psalm 110 becomes in turn the Old Testament's most quoted referent in the New Testament.

The critical effort to set the Synoptics over against the Fourth Gospel in respect to affirmation of the deity of Jesus Christ was unavailing. Even the least dogmatic of the Synoptics, the Gospel of Mark, which uses the Old Testament references sparingly, nonetheless opens with two Old Testament passages (Isa 40:3; Mal 3:1) that speak of the messenger who prepares for the historical arrival of the Lord. John the Baptist heralded "the Coming One" whom the inspired prophets had foretold (Mark 1:7-8), and Jesus' own ministry begins with the emphasis on the Kingdom of God now "at hand" (Matt 4:17; 10:7; cf. Matt 4:23; 9:35; Mark 1:14f.; Luke 4:18-21, 4:43).

Leonhard Goppelt says pointedly that in referring to the Kingdom Jesus "...was not introducing a new term. He proclaimed not that there was a Kingdom of God, but that it was now coming" (1981:1:45). The Old Testament often depicted God as King, spoke of his sovereign rule, and of his future eschatological reign. Jesus claimed to be David's lord (Mark 12:35-37) and he identified himself to the high priest in terms that precipitated a charge of blasphemy. It cannot be maintained convincingly that prior to the Gospel of John, which some on that account have dated late, we find no expression of "the essential bond between Jesus and God." For, as Goppelt notes, scattered instances are found elsewhere (in the baptismal formula of Matt 28:19, in 1 Cor 15:28, and in Heb 1:8) (1981:1:204, n.64).

More than this, the early Church worshiped Jesus not only as Lord but, as D. R. de Lacey (1982:199) stresses, as the "one Lord" (1 Cor 8:6). In short, "Paul presents a 'Christianizing' of the *shema*" (1982:200). "To Paul the lordship of Jesus is so fundamental that there is a sense in which it challenges, or at least significantly modifies, the *heis theos* to which as a Jew he was totally committed" (ibid., 201). In Oscar Cullmann's words, "early Christianity does not hesitate to transfer to Jesus everything the Old Testament says about God" (1963:307).

The weight of evidence is that Jesus believed he was God's incomparable Son, standing in God's place with divine authority and right and determining the destiny of human beings according to their response to his life and work. Radical critics contended that the claims of Jesus to be the divine Son of God originated from the early Church, while they also argued that sayings of Jesus could be considered historical if they present motifs not found in earlier Judaism. Here Jesus' claim to personal divinity would surely qualify.

To insist that the Church constructed the Jesus of the Gospels is like saying that a son has generated his own father.

Jesus expected both his approaching suffering and death, and beyond the grave, the Father's vindication of his obedient trust. This expectation was grounded not merely in a common Jewish belief in the appearance of an eschatological prophet, but in Jesus' own special redemptive mission. Jesus anticipated that vindication in a future eschatological Kingdom. But as Hans F. Bayer (1986) contends, he did not mistakenly expect the Kingdom to be introduced at his resurrection, but rather interposed a significant interim between his resurrection and his return. Contrary to the inclination of many critics to dismiss such passages, Bayer stresses the authenticity of the Gospel texts in which Jesus predicts his resurrection and vindication.

Hodgson identifies himself with what he calls "the central core" of the biblical testimony, "the belief that in Jesus Christ we see God at work in the history of the world, personally incarnate for the purpose of rescuing his creation from the evil with which it had become infected" (1968:1:82; 2:54). The Christian affirmation is not simply that "God was in Christ, reconciling the world unto himself" (2 Cor 5:19) for, Hodgson observes, these words standing alone might be compatible with the notion that God was working more fully, but not singularly and definitively, in Jesus Christ (1968:2:68). Hodgson allows, however, that "our belief in Jesus as God incarnate may have appeared in His mind as no more than a conviction of messiahship" (1968:2:89).

Hodgson jeopardizes not only the beliefs of the inspired biblical writers and his own beliefs, but those of Jesus of Nazareth also, by his insistent emphasis that human thought-forms are necessarily conditioned by the age in which one lives (1968:1:49.). Concerning Jesus, Hodgson asks: "If in Jesus Christ God was genuinely 'made man,' lived, thought and taught as the subject of experiences mediated through a body born of the Jews in Palestine not quite two thousand years ago, must we not regard His teaching as conditioned by the outlook of His time and place and racial origin?" (1968:2:89). Hodgson's answer helps us little. On the one hand, we are told that Jesus "burst the bounds" of a limited selfhood; on the other, that "we have no experience enabling us to know the extent to which perfect self-dedication to the finding and doing of God's will in a life of unbroken communion with God in the unity of the Spirit, would enable a man to deal with his own particular circumstances in such a way as to reveal principles of universal relevance" (1968:2:89). But if universal principles or truths could be revealed to and in the mind of Jesus by the Spirit, why could objective truth not also have been revealed by the Spirit to divinely inspired prophets and apostles who in the biblical record profess to give us information valid for all times and places?

This faith that Jesus is the incarnate Son of God preceded the crucifixion and resurrection of Jesus. But it was decisively confirmed by the resurrection of the Crucified One, who brought forgiveness of sins and imparted new life by the Spirit. The Book of Acts and the New Testament epistles affirm that Christ is the personal presence of God in the community of faith. The very first Christian sermon, by Peter at Pentecost, within weeks of the crucifixion of Jesus, stressed that Jesus is risen and ascended, that he has effected forgiveness of sins for the penitent, and that he has gifted the Holy Spirit to his followers. The Messiah's redemptive mission included as its "central aim," as Hodgson observes, his forming "a fellowship of forgiven sinners" (1968:2:71) despite the fact that many Jewish religious leaders spurned Jesus because they were expecting a political messiah. Messianic cancellation of personal sin was clearly a feature emphasized by John the Baptist (John 1:29) and in turn by Jesus (Mark 2:7); it had in fact been anticipated by the sacrificial system of the Old Testament economy awaiting decisive fulfillment (Heb 9:23,26). Hodgson emphasizes that Christians can justify their belief in the incarnation not merely as a matter of subjective consciousness but as a prior objective fact "if we think of what was done as having been done by God Himself" (1968:2:75).

Hodgson orients belief in the divinity of Christ too much in post-apostolic considerations, however, when he remarks: "The history of the doctrine of the Incarnation in the first four centuries is the history of the Church discovering that Jesus could not have been God's Messiah and done God's saving work without Himself being God" (1968:2:70). For that "discovery" had been made much earlier. The belief that gives the Christian confession its singularly unique character, that in Jesus Christ dwelt "all the fullness of the Godhead bodily" (Col 2:9), is an integral and definitive aspect of the New Testament teaching; it is affirmed and reiterated by the apostles who were contemporaries of Jesus. Hodgson concedes in fact that "within the New Testament period Christians were already, in practice, adopting an attitude towards Christ which implied the recognition of Him as God." But he considers it "doubtful whether these first Christians thought out the theological implications of their religious belief and practice" (1968:2:76).

That Jesus Christ was "God personally incarnate," writes Hodgson, "is the ground of the claim of Christianity to be the true religion for all mankind" (1968:2:70). Hodgson considers that the evidence for the virgin birth and resurrection of Jesus is "as good as one can reasonably expect historical evidence to be" and that one who believes the high view of Jesus Christ is justified in accepting it at its face value" (1968:2:91). But, in contrast to the creeds of Christendom, he thinks these doctrines can be detached from genuine faith in Jesus Christ as God incarnate.

But did Jesus of Nazareth then by his own faith inspire the belief of others in his messianic sonship and divinity? Does Christian faith in Jesus Christ rest finally upon the impression of Jesus' personality and on claims he made for himself? He indicated the value and limits of the Baptist's testimony without nullifying the importance of his own messianic consciousness: "I receive not testimony from man" and "I know that the witness he witnesses of me is true" (John 5:34,32).

Yet Jesus warned against claims made independently by himself or anyone else. "If I bear witness of myself, my witness is not true" (John 5:31). He set his own witness in the larger context of that of the Father, of Scripture, and of his own works (John 5:32-39).

Yet for Paul and the Gentile churches it is not Jesus' public ministry but especially his resurrection from the dead that is the historically decisive point for the Christian community. The Easter faith was, to be sure, indispensably linked to the incarnation, earthly life, and ministry of Jesus. New Testament theology nowhere justifies Bultmann's dismissal of the supernatural Jesus of history in the interest solely of an inner "resurrection" encounter. Indeed, the Gospels leave no doubt that Jesus' own intimations of his impending crucifixion and resurrection seemed confusing to the disciples and that they were both dismayed by his death and unexpectant of his resurrection. It was not their unexpected confrontation by the risen Jesus alone, but the Old Testament prophetic teaching also concerning the coming One that finally illumined Messiah's death and triumph over it in terms of divine prophecy and fulfillment.

Part 2

From Galilee
to Chalcedon

4

Coherence or Confusion?

The current critical emphasis on the christological diversity of the New Testament implies that the biblical writers hold conflicting views of Jesus Christ and that the Christian credal commitment to the divinity of the Nazarene arose gradually as a projection of the Church. We are even told, for example, that Jesus himself adduced an adoptionist model of his sonship, whereas Paul, through a process of theological debate and ecclesial consensus, provided a Second Adam model that emerged as the traditional view.

Paula Fredriksen (1988) professes to find diverse christologies in the Gospels and in the New Testament as a whole. Fredriksen can speak of the Johannine "stranger from heaven," the Lucan "messiah of the Gentiles," the Matthean "Christ of the Scriptures," the Markan "secret messiah," and the Pauline "Christ of the *parousia*" as if these were mainly remotely related imaginative reconstructions from Hellenistic antecedents. These supposedly conflicting scriptural accounts are considered the occasion of novel christologies that emerged in post-biblical history. Consequently Fredriksen rejects confidence in a unilinear development in first century Christology.

Beyond doubt, the Gospels note that some Jews considered Jesus an habitual blasphemer, that the priestly bureaucracy viewed him as an heretical disrupter of the *status quo*, and that the Roman regime executed him as an insurrectionist. But it takes an unusually fertile mind to hold that the New Testament itself espouses a society of rival Jesuses. Such an approach strips the New Testament of any objective revelatory view, deprives the Church of an "orthodox" Christology, and considers varying modern doctrines of Christianity's Founder to be theologically acceptable as long as they remain generally within the orbit of broad apostolic divergences.

That the early Christians affirmed that "Jesus is Lord" has encouraged some interpreters to seek in this pithy confession the sum and substance of New Testament faith. But, as Charles M. Wood (1981:103) insists, this brief affirmation is not sufficiently stable in meaning to state the core of Christianity apart from a literature or canon that illumines the confession. Yet Wood's own critical view of both Scripture and canon unfortunately defeats their serviceability to define the confession authoritatively.

A Consistent and Coherent Witness

One need not impose an arbitrary unity to find in the New Testament texts a consistent and coherent witness to Jesus Christ. All the canonical writings attest to his incomparable person and redemptive work. Fundamental to the New Testament message is that Jesus of Nazareth is the incarnation of the divine Logos and the one and only Son of God. On the person and work of Christ, Paul and the Jerusalem apostles were in full accord (1 Cor 15:3-11). The truth of the Christian religion is in the first and last analysis tied to the affirmation of Jesus Christ as the one incarnate divine Savior.

The contemporary emphasis on christological diversity all too readily misreads vocabulary divergences as logical differences. As Clark Pinnock remarks, "It is precarious to assume that because Paul felt it proper to describe Christ in terms of wisdom and John to describe him in terms of *logos* they were somehow contradicting each other," since such affirmations are "entirely compatible" (1982:60). Pinnock further stresses that the New Testament writers do not in all circumstances convey the entirety of their beliefs. If we had exhaustive access to their views, he suggests, we might find that at times they deliberately omitted the reiteration of what other apostles had already stressed, and that they were concerned to supplement rather than to duplicate their emphases. Such argument from silence is, to be sure, always precarious. While avoidance of reiteration might indeed at times have been a consideration, the fact that not all of the apostolic epistles were accessible in all places, and that some were addressed to specific congregations or readers, counts against it. But Pinnock is right, nonetheless, when he says that to affirm contrary christologies in the New Testament is tantamount to postulating conflicting gospels, since the portrait of Christ is central to the New Testament.

Against recent New Testament scholars who overstress diversity, Donald Guthrie (1981:54-55) insists that the person, work, and mission of Jesus Christ in fact comprise unifying factors in New Testament theology. Contrary to those who project radical differences between Johannine and Synoptic christology, Guthrie contends that "the Johannine Son of man teaching... accords completely with the synoptics' presentation, that it presents both heavenly and earthly aspects,... that it is in harmony with other expressions of Christology in the gospel... (and) is an important link in the view that a basic unity exists between the synoptic and Johannine approach to Christology" (1981:287).

James Dunn's view that New Testament christology is diverse and that its various christologies have little cohesion other than a concurrence that the Risen Lord is the Jesus of history is flawed (1977). While recognizing the interlocking ways the New Testament writers assessed the significance of Jesus, Dunn nevertheless tends to mistake complementarity for contradiction and accommodates a confusing range of selectivity and subjectivism in interpretation (1980:8). That there is theological development is undebatable; indeed, it is a necessary feature of progressive revelation. But the writers are not on that account to be considered as necessarily at odds with each other.

Jesus is "understood in the New Testament... as God's conclusive revelation," says Leonhard Goppelt (1981:1:280). Against those who mainly emphasize a diversity of witness in the accounts, Goppelt declares to be "fundamental" for its self-understanding the fact that the New Testament "wishes to attest a fulfillment event coming from the God of the Old Testament and having Jesus at its center" (ibid., 281).

The critical schools' emphasis on the supposed irreconcilable diversity of the accounts often reflects a deep prejudice against supernatural transcendence and miraculous divine manifestation. Once the incarnation is dismissed *a priori* as an impossibility, no logical or consistent witness to its factuality is expected and the pursuit of deviations becomes the order of the day.

Paul Knitter, a Roman Catholic who imposes a myth-hermeneutic upon Scripture, insists that Christianity does not affirm the finality and superiority of God's revelation in Christ. Christians need not regard the incarnation as a factual, historical once-for-all event, he declares; Lord Buddha, Lord Krishna, and Lord Jesus are but parallel perspectives (1979:651-71). But Avery Dulles (1985:190) pointedly replies that "fidelity to the Christian confession...excludes the idea that there is any Lord except Jesus (cf. 1 Cor. 8:6)." The reduction of the Gospels merely to sacred narrative permits Stephen Crites (1981:178) also to accommodate a mythologizing of the incarnation. The gospel of the resurrection is "that God is fully present in this story" apart from "a God-man as such, mythic or otherwise." John Hick (1977:14) promotes the critical prejudice plainly when in the preface to a recent symposium he tells us that any identification of Jesus "as God incarnate, the Second Person of the Holy Trinity living a human life, is a mythological or poetic way of expressing his significance for us." Hick declares the statement that Jesus was "the Son of God incarnate" not only "literally untrue" but without factual meaning. He considers the creeds to be carriers of myth. Says Hick: "The Christian mind will almost inevitably come to see the doctrine of the resurrection, and the doctrine of the Trinity which grew out of it, in a new way, no longer as precise metaphysical truths but as imaginative constructions giving expression...to the Christian's devotion to Jesus as the one who has made the heavenly Father real to him" (1980:125).

In his short contribution to *The Myth of God Incarnate*, Don Cupitt (1977) looks upon worship of Christ as a paganization of Christianity, indeed, as essentially idolatrous. He suggests that early Christianity, after it repudiated the Roman Emperor-cult, refocused imperial worship on Jesus. Cupitt voices an unhesitating 'no' to the question whether we may identify the Jesus of history as also the divine Christ, God's incarnate Son (1979:145). But Cupitt ignores, as Geoffrey Wainwright notes, that it was in view of its earlier affirmation that "Jesus is Lord" that Christianity rejected the Emperor-cult, and that Christians declared Christ not only Lord but also divine Judge of the earth before whom all finite authorities would bow the knee (1980:277-78).

Charles Davis (1976:87-88) somewhat similarly views traditional Christology as "a remarkable achievement of the creative imagination as it strove to express the experience of the transcendent." Such representations clearly transmute the historic creeds into literary fiction.

Hendrikus Berkhof dismisses the virgin birth and ascension of Jesus as figments of late tradition and espouses at best an adoptionist view of the divine Christ (1979:287-88, 293, 310-12.). The New Testament, he says, knows nothing of an extra-human Jesus (ibid., 288). Berkhof only partly spells out the dire implications of his further insistence that the humanness of Scripture necessarily involves its error and contradiction (ibid., 87-88). For if whatever is human is therefore inescapably fallible, not only all that Scripture tells us about Jesus but Jesus' own human nature as well would then necessarily bear the marks of fallibility. Berkhof only verbally escapes the consistent implications of a fallible humanity for his own representations.

Is the person identified by the New Testament as Jesus of Nazareth really the one and only Messiah, the incarnate Logos through whom a possibility of salvation arises for the seditious human race? Was Simon Peter right when to Jewish elders and Palestinian rulers he declared that "no other name" under heaven is given among men whereby we must be saved (Acts 4:12)? Does the truth of Christianity associated with the name and work of Jesus, a christological claim relative to one specific religious heritage, express also a universal principle—a possibility of human healing and rescue not necessarily linked to a specific person or tradition, but reflected no less in a divine manifestation in Buddha and other religious personalities offering their own individual paths to enlightenment? Could the self-same person whom his Christian followers affirm to be the Christ have manifested himself elsewhere under divergent names, so that humans in other traditions relate themselves unknowingly to the Jesus of the Bible, who meets them existentially and savingly in their faith?

In whatever variety of ways God might reveal himself, does it not seem least possible, or at any rate least likely, that he would come in the nature of a babe that wore diapers and grew into a particular man with long hair and bushy eyebrows, and who wept and thirsted, suffered pangs of crucifixion, and truly died? Who has not shared Augustine's early doubts about the very credibility of all this (*The Confessions of St. Augustine*, 5:10)? Does not the thought seem even more mad in our own century than it did two millenniums ago when, as G. K. Chesterton put it, "his own nation...lynched him,...shuddering at his earth-shaking blasphemies" (cited in E. A. Waycock, 1963:189). Does it not seem incredible on the very surface that this babe, born in a manger, would be the most influential person in the universe and remain even today the most powerful?

Was "the 'grammatical monstrosity' the God-man," as some portray it, merely a conceptual antecedent of Superman? Even Nietzsche's Superman also transcends mankind—albeit in a way that reduces the entire human species to mediocrity and derides the Christian virtues of humaneness, sympathy, and pity.

As the very incarnation of *agape*, Jesus was neither effeminate nor, as Michael Novak notes, was he given to warlike and martial virtues (1983:67). Would the scandal have been at all diminished had he not been born of a woman, or even had the Nazarene come as woman rather than as man? Or if Messiah had come as pure spirit, neither male nor female, garbed perhaps in angelic nature without any physical body?

Does it not remain a scandal among secular philosophers that the one so ignominiously executed was the eternal Christ who emptied himself of the marks of status which were his by right (George Carey, 1978:34) and became obedient to the Father in his sinless life and substitutionary death for sinners?

Yet Christianity has heralded that good news to the intervening centuries, and without apology. If Jesus in truth claimed divinity, he alone could and did move among the masses in a way that maintained that claim. The works he performed and the life he then lived did not appear supernatural to him; the supernatural is supernatural only to the natural. He lived at once the most natural and supernatural life, in that he alone lived up to the full possibility of ideal human nature, and in that he performed signs and made promises that he knew to be the sole prerogative of deity.

"The church's paramount message about history," writes Herbert Schlossberg, "is that the dividing line between B.C. and A.D. is not just a convention...the coming of Jesus Christ into history is the manifestation of eternity into time" (1983:51). "The figure who furnished the history of Christianity with its fundamental continuity has been Jesus Christ," comments William Clebsch (1979:13). "Always and everywhere Christians have named him their Savior and made him the model for their religiousness" (ibid.). The fact is that no one more than Jesus of Nazareth has fixed for the Western world the decisive meaning of the reality of God. From its early days, in Aramaic no less than in Greek, the Christian community confessed Jesus as "Lord" (Acts 2:36; 1 Cor 1:21; 16:22).

Modern Confusion Over Christology

Yet, more than any other century since Christian beginnings, our century seems confused over the identity of Jesus and unsure even of what the Nazarene thought of himself and of his role in the world. Robert W. Jensen remarked in an unpublished essay on Jonathan Edwards' christology that "the root weakness of America's Christianity has been its christological fragility," and others have commented on the zig-zag course of modern christology as a whole. In *The Present-Day Christological Debate* (1984) Klaas Runia assesses thirteen recent christologies mainly of Continental origin.

Anglo-Saxon liberal christology was notably fashioned against the background of a century of continental German criticism. But as a movement, as J. S. Lawton says, English theology resisted the more radical christological views for which many continental theologians exhibited a preference (1943:7). Alister E. McGrath surveys German christology since the Enlightenment and devotes almost a chapter to Barth, Bultmann, Pannenberg, Moltmann, and Jungel that channels their differences into a progressive development. McGrath's perspective is clear: the relationship between revelation and history is at stake in the conflict over christology. "Either something is history, and open to historical investigation, or it does not exist: there is no alternative" (1986:3). The christologies of Schleiermacher, Ritschl, Barth, and Tillich are flawed, he insists, because they inadequately face this issue. While McGrath thinks better of Bultmann, Moltmann, and Jungel for not wholly evading the matter, he unfortunately does not rule on the adequacy of their solutions. McGrath's concern is to maintain the link between "the historical figure of Jesus of Nazareth with the Christ of the *Kerygma*" (1986:153). Important as that is, it does not decisively answer the question of the identity of Jesus. We dare not hedge the question whether the Jesus that historical criticism postulates is also the Jesus of the Gospels.

There are still classical liberals who, more than a half century behind the times, seem unfamiliar with the challenge that serious scholarship has posed to radical biblical criticism, skeptical form-criticism, and redaction criticism (cf. Ronald Nash, 1984:4). They repeat the now outworn reconceptualizations of Jesus—as does Thomas Sheehan (1986), a noncatholic philosopher at Loyola University in Chicago— that Jesus was merely a fallible prophet, not virgin-born, made no divine claims, founded no religion akin to Christianity, and is as dead as any corpse can be.

Bernard Cooke notes that a growing number of Roman Catholic scholars now tend to make Christian experience the starting point of theological reflection, thereby reducing the role of an authoritative Scripture. In such exposition all dogmatic affirmations are understood in the context of Christian faith out of which they are said to arise. He draws the obvious conclusion that no basic christological consensus any longer exists. Christian belief—even about Jesus Christ—is therefore easily redefined as "an unfolding reality whose multiplicities are intrinsic to tradition" (1990:216).

Jesus is meanwhile heralded by New Age prophets as the harbinger of the 'new age' of self-realization, love, and world peace" implicit in our latent divinity. New Age scribe John White depicts Jesus as the West's model of "cosmic consciousness," the "incarnation of a higher intelligence and ground of being, of a universal energy to which we must link our lives"

(1989:14). He is "a god-realized man," not "the final incarnation of the Creation" (Douglas Groothuis, (1990:221). The "New Age Christ" is an omnipresent cosmic principle that aims to raise humanity to new evolutionary heights (David Spangler, 1978:107).

Rosemary Reuther meanwhile claims that the New Testament leads by a short line to the Nazi Holocaust. The Christian church, she contends, bears "substantial responsibility" for the political anti-Semitism on which the Nazis built (1974:184). Frank Musser (1981) contends that the early Christian writings revise the Jesus materials and exploit the conflict between Christianity and Judaism through the claim that God has rejected the Jews, thus promoting a prideful self-centered Christian alternative. But does New Testament christology breed the Holocaust as its inevitable consequence? Is anti-Semitism, as Reuther implies, the logical underside of the affirmations that Jesus is the Christ (1974:64-66)? Robert T. Osborn puts the question well: "To be pro-Christ, must one be anti-Jew?"

Reuther proposes to overcome anti-Semitism by rejecting any claim to religious exclusivity by Judaism and Christianity. That solution, as Osborn rightly recognizes, involves a denial of the essence of these religions. "Christian anti-Judaism has its roots," Osborn replies, "not in Christian faith but in Christian faithlessness" (1985:341). One might add that the faithlessness that disavows the singular uniqueness of revealed religion leads by a short line to a clouding of the biblical virtues of justice and love.

Osborn identifies as Christian blasphemy the tendency of some Christian expositors to deny the Jewishness of Jesus. To view Jesus as the universal man, but not as a particular Jew, he holds, gives theology a functional anti-Semitic proclivity. Both the incarnate and resurrected Christ are Jewish, insists Osborn, however much wider may be the significance of Jesus' mission and ministry; Christ belongs to both Israel and the Church (cf. Rom 11:17-18). The notion that the rise of the Christian Church cancels God's covenant promise to Abraham, he says, overlooks the fact that Gentiles must become Israel's adopted children, even as Israel now must find salvation in the Church.

The readiness of many Jews today to discuss the affirmation of Jesus' messianity and divinity as a cultic Gentile development wholly ignores the fact that Christian faith emerged first within the Jewish community prior to Gentile involvement. It was pious Jews, devoted to their biblical heritage and awaiting their promised Messiah, who first affirmed that Jesus is the divine Savior for Jew and Gentile alike. Jewish disfavor for Jesus often forgets how much the Jewish community itself, and Judaism with it, has changed since the early Christian era. Whereas Christians are now frequently charged with having altered the inherited view of messianity, Jewish religious leaders themselves promoted alternatives to traditional Jewish doctrines and practices that early messianic churches retained [cf. Cyrus H. Gordon, (1983:665-90)]. If the term "messiah" as Christians currently use it is unrecognizable by modern Jews, the cause does not rest solely with Gentile Christianity. Christian Jews have not really had to disavow their Jewishness to become Christians. One of the most notable Christian Jews, Jean-Marie Cardinal Lustiger, whose relatives were destroyed at Auschwitz, was named archbishop of Paris. He became a believer through reading the Bible, and he wrote: "I found Judaism's fulfillment in welcoming Jesus, the Messiah of Israel. . . . I am not ceasing to be a Jew; on the contrary, I am discovering another way of being a Jew" (1986:41-42).

Revival of Evangelical Engagement

The day is now gone when evangelical scholars can be fairly charged with neglecting christology. The numerous contributors to *Christ the Lord* (1982) indicates the growing evangelical interest in christological themes. The bibliography volume compiled by Leland Jennings White on *Jesus the Christ* (1988), impressive as it is, reflects only a part of that interest. The growing literature includes works by Harold O. J. Brown (1984); H. Dermot McDonald (1968); Leon Morris (1987); Bernard Ramm (1985); John Stott (1985); Douglas A. Webster (1987); David Wells (1984); and Millard Erickson (1991). They share the conviction that Christianity confronts the worldly wise with a threefold scandal: that God calls sinners to repentance rather than exalting the self-righteous, that God manifests his glory supremely in the man Christ Jesus rather than in a theophany of pure spirit, and that God is the eternal One-and-Three rather than a metaphysical monad.

For an orthodox Christian, the most important phrase in all intellectual history is that "the Word became flesh" (John 1:14). Central to christological controversy remains the issue whether Jesus Christ is a man only or whether he is properly understood only as God manifest in flesh. That a man might become God is absurd; that God might become God-man is clearly not so. Can Christ really be our substitute unless he was fully human? Can he be the one and only Savior of humankind if he is but a human being? If he is supernatural in his salvific work, can he truly be so unless he also is supernatural in person? In short, who is the Savior and what is the nature of the salvation he offers? The answer is not made easier by the fact that, as R. T. France (1982:27) remarks, Jesus did not go around "proclaiming himself to be God."

James Dunn (1980) professes to give us a historical summary of the way the concept of divine incarnation in Jesus originated and was developed in the New Testament literature. This he does by surveying the titles and other conceptions used by Jesus' early followers to express his significance. The referents Son of God, Son of Man, last Adam, the Wisdom and Word of God, and the Spirit- and Angel-christologies are assessed beginning with the Old Testament foregleams, the self-testimony of Jesus, the apostolic *kerygma*, then the epistles of Paul, the Synoptics, Hebrews and, finally the writings of John.

As a rule Dunn finds in the earliest New Testament formulations references only to Jesus' eschatological transcendence, while in the later materials alone does he find any affirmation of Christ's personal preexistence and creative activity. He emphasizes that Jesus' resurrection held the central role in early Christian thought. His verdict is that the line of christological development in early Christianity led progressively from an initial affirmation of Jesus' eschatological and/or resurrection sonship to the claim of divine transcendence also in his death, and then in his earthly ministry and life, and subsequently in his birth also, until at last the climax was reached of a claim to divine personal preexistence.

Dunn finds no pre-Christian evidence for the concept of a divine son descending to earth to become man in order to bring salvation. He traces the Synoptic tradition to Jesus and attributes to him a unique sense that anticipates his Son of God eschatological representation of the Father. The Christian *kerygma*, he holds, ascribes Jesus' transcendence and divine sonship to his resurrection from the dead. But Paul considers Jesus the divine Son even in his death. Hebrews then introduces his divine preexistence, but only as a Platonic (or more directly Philonic) idea in the divine mind. Only John rises to affirm the personal preexistence of the Son who descended from heaven to become flesh. Dunn concludes that, late in the first century, John welded the philosophical concept of an impersonal preexisting Logos-principle to the theological concept of divine sonship to produce the view of Jesus as a divinely preexistent person who becomes man for the sake of our salvation.

Dunn's conclusions have been routinely and quite properly criticized along several lines. For one thing, he pursues evidence for belief in divine incarnation on the premise that Christianity disallows the concept of a person "independent" of God. This confuses Old Testament data where the Angel of the Lord and the Wisdom of God appear at times as at once God and yet as God beside God. The same prejudiced notion of independent selfhood encourages Dunn to criticize John as risking a compromise of Hebrew monotheism (1980:264-65).

A related problem arises from Dunn's disposition to level the teaching of the New Testament texts to conceptions prevalent initially in first-century non-Christian Hebrew and Hellenic circles. Although he concedes that the biblical writers could have made singular claims for Jesus, he preferably opts for the contemporary non-Christian horizon so that Christ's incarnation is deleted as a theme in the great kenosis passage Phil 2:6-11 (1980:114-15) and references to Christ's agency in creation (e.g., 1 Cor 8:6; Col 1:15-20) are reinterpreted to evacuate that sense.

The conclusion to which Dunn's understanding of the Pauline

texts leads is that firm evidence is nonexistent that the great Apostle to the Gentiles affirmed Christ's personal preexistence and incarnation. But to reduce the meaning of Col 1:15-20 to "the writer's... saying that Christ now reveals the character of the power behind the world" (1980:190) is an unjustifiable dilution. Dennis Johnson penetratingly asks: If, as Dunn contends, "John could make a claim for Jesus in his prologue which moved decisively beyond anything Philo had claimed for the Logos, could not Paul have introduced his churches to the concept of Christ as personally active in creation, even though such a concept moved beyond Stoic and Jewish descriptions of Wisdom?" (1982:168).

Dunn's thesis, that belief in Christ's pre-existence emerges only after the apostle Paul, is refuted by many writers (e.g. Seyoon-Kim, 1981). That Christ became human does not mean that he became an incarnate adult, but rather that the eternal Logos ventured a reality that began with conception in the womb—and proceeded through infancy and childhood to maturity, thereby to be linked to a stream of ancestry that reaches back through Mary to Abraham and Noah and Adam.

Flight to the Mythical

The identification of Jesus of Nazareth as the God-man is increasingly avoided today on the simple presupposition and prejudice that the Gospel accounts are narrative myth. Much of the impetus for this confusion of genre is due to the influence of Rudolf Bultmann, who existentialized New Testament theology and, in view of a nineteenth century cosmology that viewed nature as a seamless causal network, declared the Gospels to be unhistorical and considered their representations a product of the post-apostolic church. In his view, Jesus was only a human being who lived in Palestine, taught in parables, perhaps healed the sick, and died. Except for a waning cadre of Bultmann's disciples this "Bultmannian myth," as the Norwegian scholar Oskar Skarsaune labels it, "has disintegrated and virtually disappeared from debate" (1991:132). "Few scholarly positions," comments Skarsaune, "have had to endure such treatment in recent research" as has Bultmann's dismissal of the New Testament picture in terms of a correlation of Jewish apocalypticism with the Gnostic myth of redemption (ibid.).

Burton L. Mack, influenced by the French structuralist Michel Foucault, views the New Testament writings in terms of Christian myth and symbol (1988). While many critical documentary theorists have long considered Mark's Gospel most reliable, Mack declares that even Mark does not reliably portray the history of Jesus. He adds that John's Gospel contains elements aiming to present Jesus as an epic figure in the mythic history of the Jews (ibid., 54), while Paul assertedly invents resurrection appearances (1 Cor 15:5-7) to establish his own authority. What remains of Jesus is a Cynic-like teacher armed with proverbs and parables. In short, we are left with literary fiction in the name of authentic history. It is unsurprising that Mack concludes by dismissing the messianic motif entirely (ibid., 376). What is tragic is that he grotesquely deforms the New Testament in order to pacify his unbelief.

While historical events happen but once, Christianity by the once-for-all events of the Bible, notably the incarnation of God in Jesus Christ, claims much more than the singularity we attach to other events. The uniqueness Christianity assigns to Jesus is not relative but absolute, a uniqueness decisive for all humankind, a category of being that admits of no comparisons, one involving an unprecedented and incomparable relationship between Godhead and humanity, in which Jesus Christ is the only one "of the Father's kind."

Thomas Boslooper holds that Christianity projected the virgin birth of Jesus as a biblical legend that "established a natural bridge between the Christian community and non-Christian society. The closest association between Christian and pagan tradition was at the point of the narratives of the birth of gods and heroes" (1962:234). The virgin birth doctrine differed from the pagan myths in that Jesus was a real human, but it carried the seed of the doctrine of divine incarnation, or the unity of God and man in Christ, which creeds misunderstand, Boslooper contends, in terms of the deity of Christ.

The ancient religions, secular anthropologists remind us, often have "gods who become human." Yet nothing here really coincides with the biblical doctrine of divine incarnation in Jesus of Nazareth. The one living God of the Bible is not interchangeable with these "gods," nor even in a temporary episode is the God-man simply "human." To be sure, the Olympian mythical deities temporarily transmute themselves into humans, but Jacques Ellul rightly calls this "amusing ribaldry." Venus turns into a woman because she wants to sleep with a certain man; Jupiter turns himself into Amphytrion so he can play tricks on human beings. Jupiter also metamorphoses into a bull and a swan (shades of a doctrine of transmigration more than of incarnation or reincarnation?). Where does one find here, asks Ellul, an essential element of the biblical doctrine, namely "the continuous working out of a plan, like that of the God of Israel?" (1983:98).

Martin Hengel notes that "the Greek gods are born and have human pleasures (sometimes even with human beings), but they can never die, their bodily form is only 'show'" (1976:40). The ancient world, he adds, has no analogy to the crucifixion of a presumed Jewish criminal who is a preexistent divine figure who voluntarily assumes human form to die upon the cross the most shameful death known to antiquity (ibid., 1). "The incarnation of a divine figure and still more his shameful death on the cross was not a 'point of contact'" with Greek premises but rather "a 'scandal' and a 'stumbling block'" (ibid., 41; cf. A. D. Nock, , 1972:2:93-335). There is moreover "no gnostic redeemer myth," says Hengel, "which can be demonstrated chronologically to be pre-Christian" (1976:33).

Beyond doubt Jesus Christ remains a powerful symbol in much of modern society. But no mere mythological or existential unpacking of that symbol will do. It is unsurprising that Robert F. Berkey (1982:22) thinks that the numerous failed approaches of the now closing century have the effect of "forcing us back to the christological drawing board."

For Greek and Roman thought it was conceivable that a human could be divinized; what was outside the range of possibility was that God should assume human nature, since matter was thought to be evil. In the Bible, by contrast, humans have no latent potential whatever for divinity. The core message of Christianity is that "the Word became flesh"

(John 1:14), i.e., that the eternal Logos assumed human nature, albeit without divesting himself of divine nature. For Old Testament thought it was inconceivable that God should become a human (Hos 11:9; cf. Num 23:19; Ezek 28:2, 9). The mutual exclusiveness of the divine and the human as distinct ontological categories is as characteristic of the New Testament as of the Old (Acts 5:29). But the Johannine prologue does not say that the Word *became man*, as if an exchange of ontological essence was involved. The Logos assumes human nature without divestiture of the divine. And the Logos, while divine, is not the entirety of the Godhead, albeit nonetheless the essentially divine second person of the Trinity.

Skarsaune contends that the New Testament doctrine of once-for-all divine incarnation in Jesus Christ did not arise from a Hellenistic nonbiblical environment nor did it arise from the prevalent Jewish view of Messiah. Both those sources considered divine incarnation in human flesh an ontological impossibility. Greek anti-mythology philosophy held that God cannot suffer or be powerless, hence the human Jesus could not be identified with deity. The prevalent Hebrew concept of Messiah anticipated that a strictly human being would be the designated Messiah. The biblical Creator-creature distinction would also tend to view a God-Man doctrine as offensive.

The crucial link to once-for-all divine incarnation Skarsaune finds in the doctrine of Wisdom (Old Testament) and Christ (New Testament) as pre-existent divine agent in creation. The Old Testament expounded the Wisdom, Word, and Spirit of God not in terms merely of personification, and the conception of Wisdom gained fullest significance in its transfer to Jesus. Long before Jesus' time true Judaism spoke "of 'personified' (hypostatized) aspects of God serving as 'agents' or 'acting authorities' for God" (1991:47-48). What was offensive to Hebrew theology was not an implied plurality within the divine essence, says Skarsaune, but "the overstepping of the boundary between God and humanity which the incarnation implied" (ibid., 48). Jesus claimed to be more than the messenger or bearer of wisdom. Even as in the Old Testament, Wisdom calls humanity to herself, and not to God in distinction from herself, so also Jesus portrays himself, as John F. Balchin notes, as Wisdom (1982:218).

In John's Gospel, as Raymond Brown reminds us, Wisdom is a key that exhibits the principle operations of the Logos: preexistence, participation in creation, entry into a hostile world, creation of the children of God, the world's incomprehension, rejection by her own (1966:519-24). Yet not unlike Paul in 1 Cor 2:24, John uses not Sophos/Sophia but Logos. His view is logocentric: The Logos has metaphysical transcendence, being outside the universe and time, yet stepping into the world.

Skarsaune finds in the New Testament no traces whatever of a conflict between Hebrew monotheism and Christian faith in Jesus' divinity, contrary to the view presently dominating historical theology. There was, he thinks, no controversy "differentiating between dissimilar attributes of God as though God had an inner structure." Yet the questions arise whether one can glide so easily from a plurality of divine attributes to a plurality of divine persons, and whether a controversy over monotheism is not really involved, for example, in John 5:17 in view of Jesus' claim that God is his very own Father, which he reinforces to unbelieving Jews by emphasizing that he exercises the prerogatives of deity. Yet Skarsaune's insistence that the doctrine of the incarnation of God in Christ is not a speculative evolutionary development of nonbiblical thought, but that it has firm anticipation in the revelatory literature of the Old Testament helps to restore balance to the discussion of Christology.

5

Jesus as God Incarnate

Christology "from Above" or "from Below"?

The debate over whether christology should be pursued *von oben* ("from above") or *von unten* ("from below") is settled by the New Testament which accords a proper role to both. The Gospel of Mark reflects the growing conviction of the disciples that Jesus is the Christ: Jesus is recognized as a uniquely authoritative teacher (1:27), who forgives sins (2:7), who commands the wind and waves (4:41), who is confessed as the Christ (8:21), who will enter into his glory (10:37; cf. John 20:31). The Gospel of John and the Pauline Epistles place the reality of the incarnation in the larger context of his eternal preexistent divinity: The Christ is Jesus and Jesus Christ is Lord (John 1:1; Acts 2:26; 5:42; 9:22; 16:31; 18:5; 18:28; 1 Cor. 12:3; Phil. 2:11).

The current critical emphasis on christology "from below" commendably seeks to do justice to the historical Jesus whom the disciples came to confess as Lord. But some of its promoters aim to escape what they depict pejoratively as a static view of divine being, a mythical supernatural worldview, and a "three-deck cosmology" that represents the Son as "coming down" from heaven. The prevalent approach seeks Jesus' divinity through his humanity, and then defines his uniqueness only in terms of a difference of degree rather than of kind. Inevitably, therefore, it distorts the biblical concept of incarnation. Yet, as Colin E. Gunton notes, the real problem that "Christology from above" poses for contemporary thought lies in the modern assumption of a completely immanent universe declared to be wholly in the grip of time; consequently, eternity and divine transcendence become problematical (1983). The modern protest against static being,

Gunton stresses, can be defanged by quotations from patristic fathers that show these current complaints to be unfounded. The fathers, he affirms, moved away from ancient Greek dualism to the notion of *pericleonesis* (the being and indwelling of each of the three persons in the others) and anticipated a view approaching the recent emphasis of philosophy of science on mutual atomic penetration of the realms of existence.

Theology "from below," observes David Wells, "yields only a larger-than-life religious figure, the perfection of what many others already experience" (1984:172). The contemporary danger therefore becomes that of readily misjudging what is meant both by full deity and full humanity. As currently pursued, Christology "from below" yields no consensus. The conflicting inferences stretch from Pannenberg's *Jesus—God and Man* to Peter Hodgson's *Jesus— Word and Presence* (1971), and do not, by any means, stop there.

Edward Schillebeeckx (1979) pursues the man of Nazareth through historical inquiry, considers absolutizing any event a false option, and avoids any objective affirmation of the deity of Christ. In a movement that shifts christology from the Word incarnate to the obedient Jesus and focuses on quantitative rather than qualitative differences between Jesus and humanity in general, he obscures the role of the eternal Son during the incarnation. He runs the risk, some critics reply, of elevating contemporary existential-shaped experience into a "fifth Gospel" that provides its own categories for the understanding of Jesus.

The worship of Jesus did not arise only with apostolic Christianity, stresses R. T. France, and far less did it emerge through the influence of exotic mythological notions. In *Christ the Lord* (ed. Rowden) France notes that:

> The incarnational Christology of the New Testament had its roots not in philosophical speculation, and still less in the gra tuitous imitation of supposedly similar ideas in other religions and cultures, but in Christian experience of Jesus, both in his earthly ministry and in his risen power.... The natural translation of this experience into an attitude of worship... provided the seedbed for New Testament Christology (1982:33).

France thinks that the Gospels "do not provide clear a response to what they had seen and heard during his ministry" (p. 27). Worship of Jesus, in France's view, sprang initially from an overwhelming compulsion of the disciples, despite their deep and abiding monotheism, to recognize and affirm Jesus not only as more than a man, but as worthy also of divine adoration and obedience.

Jesus' use of "Father/Son language" implied God-relationships different in kind from those of even his most devout disciples. Critics often dismiss Matt 11:27 as untypical because of its affirmation of an exclusive Father-Son relationship, yet this statement only makes explicit what is elsewhere implicit in Jesus' teaching, both in the Synoptic accounts and in the Johannine record. Jesus affirms divine prerogatives, and does so moreover in the very face of his adversaries' charges of blasphemy. France notes, as have many commentators, that Jesus claims not only the right to forgive sins (Mark 2:1-12; cf. Luke 23:34) and the prerogative of final judgment of all mankind (John 5:22f.; cf. Matt 7:21-23; 25:31-46), but declares also that he has life in himself (John 5:26; cf. 1:4). From other Hebrew teachers, even the prophets, he differs in that he teaches on his own authority (Matt 7:28-29; cf. "Amen, Amen, I say unto you") and, moreover, assigns to his teaching the enduring validity of the Word of God (Mark 13:31). To accept or to reject him is to accept or reject God (Matt 10:40; Luke 10:16). He invokes Old Testament texts in a way that unobtrusively yet unmistakably puts him in God's place on the assumption that they are one (cf. Matt 21:15-16; 25:31-34; Luke 20:13-18).

In discussing the work of Christ ahead of the person of Christ, modern theologians like Harnack, Bultmann, Bousset, Tillich, Pannenberg, and Marxsen, as Thomas C. Oden notes, run counter to the classical Christian exegetes (1989:17). The classical exegetes realized that only after establishing the identity of the Nazarene could one speak properly and adequately about his work. The attempts to develop a christology "*von unten,* from below, i.e., through history," Oden comments, "are due to be succeeded by a recovery of classic Christological exegesis on its own terms, unintimidated by modernity" (ibid., 533).

Bernard Ramm's christology commends *von oben* christological affirmation in contrast to the prevalent critical *von unten* approach. In insisting on Christ's preexistence, incarnation, virgin birth, salvific atonement, bodily resurrection, ascension, and future return, he relies on the Gospel witness with such consistency and confidence that his rejection elsewhere of an inerrant Scriptural authority seems strange.

The Three-in-One God

W. Waite Willis, Jr., emphasizes that trinitarian theism even today remains the most forceful challenge to atheism and to the endless variety of philosophical theisms espoused by mediating scholars (1987). A significant trinitarian view, one that escapes logical inconsistency and doctrinal deformity, affirms that the one God is self-manifested, not simply in three successive epochs or in three successive forms, but that the one God is immanently and eternally triune, and that he is essentially three eternal persons in one divine essence. The New Testament affirms the simultaneous yet distinct life and work of Father, Son, and Spirit.

Glossing over the biblical intimations of three eternal, co-existing divine persons in the one divine essence, often temporarily accommodates a unipersonal God whose manifestation alone is depicted as trinitarian: God the Father is viewed as divine creational activity, God the Son as incarnational or redemptive activity, and God the Spirit as internal reconciling activity. So Hans Kung (1976:476) reinterprets the Trinity functionally: as Father God is "*above* me," as Son he is "*beside* me," and as Spirit he is "*in* me." But the unsteady character of American unitarianism is attested by surveys like David Robinson's *The Unitarians and the Universalists* (1985) and Sydney E. Ahlstrom and Jonathan S. Carey's *An American Reformation: A Documentary History of Unitarian Christianity* (1985). The now prevalent Unitarian view is avowedly a deterioration of earlier representations by Joseph Priestley and W. E. Channing, who granted that Jesus' remarkable works were supernatural while insisting that his person was not.

Denial of an essential or ontological Trinity in the interest of a merely functional or economic Trinity, has sooner or later led to a total forfeiture of all trinitarian claims and beyond that to a relapse to thoroughgoing unitarianism. As Robert Preus remarks, "Throughout the history of doctrine when theologians have denied that the Father, Son and Holy Spirit are persons, they have also lost the doctrine of the immanent Trinity just as surely as when they deny the deity of the three persons" (1986:20). This deterioration is evident in the earlier modern theology of post-Enlightenment thinkers, Socinians and Unitarians, in that of nineteenth century dogmaticians like Schleiermacher, Ritschl, and Harnack, and in recent cults such as Jehovah's Witnesses. But it has not stopped there.

From a welcome for trinitarian doctrine as acceptable only in an Hegelian form—three modes of one person—recent modern theology has proceeded to a frank denial that the New Testament contains this version even in epitome, and then to a total loss of divine personality. Surrender of a trinitarian ontology leads at last to a comprehensive restatement of the scriptural gospel. David Wells notes that in our day trinitarian doctrine is frequently discussed quite apart from the issue of whether or not it responds to "an ineradicable part of biblical revelation" (1984:152).

As the theological decline from Christian ontology proceeds, the attacks on trinitarian doctrine become more and more intense. John Hick (1973), for example, deplores trinitarianism as a dispensable religious myth; to take it literally is to champion an unacceptable exclusivism (1973). Hick is, of course, right in discerning the exclusivism of trinitarian doctrine, but his dogmatic dismissal of it as myth is no less exclusive, and unjustifiably so.

Robert W. Jenson holds that orthodox formulations of God as "one essence and three persons" in actuality "communicate nothing whatsoever" (1984:143-45). The Trinity, he assures us, "is simply the Father and the man Jesus and their Spirit as the spirit of the believing community" (ibid., 155). Jenson seeks to assign trinitarian significance to Jesus by declaring that the Son is "epistemologically prior" in the movement of divine personhood (1982:167). "The temporal Jesus is a second identity in God, without need for a metaphysical double," Jenson tells us. Christ's deity, moreover, is "a final

outcome" in the eschatological future, not an eternal fact
(ibid., 140, 146). Trinitarian metaphysics here is so burdened
with conjectural philosophy that mythological creativity out-
weighs biblical data. Jenson resists a process-philosophy
exposition of trinitarianism, yet considers God's reality an
"event." But if God is not timeless (ibid., 138) and is one
event among other events, his endurance even into the eschatological future seems unassured.

Paul Van Buren, long a spokesman for the "death of God"
school, rejects the traditional view as unavoidably tritheistic
(1980:88-89). Trevor Williams reconstructs the Trinity spe-
ulatively in evolutionary terms and sets the Christian faith
in the context of a polarity of form and vitality. He depicts
Jesus as the form of God and the Spirit as the vitality of God
(1958:48). Cyril C. Richardson declares the doctrine of the
Trinity "an artificial construct" (ibid.). Harvey Cox's *Many
Mansions: A Christian's Encounter with Other Faiths* (1988)
leaves the Christian doctrine of the Trinity wholly in midair.

Ronald F. Thiemann acknowledges that Matthew's narrative identifies God in "a relation of differentiated unity" of
Father, Son, and Spirit and thus contains "the elements for
the subsequent development" of trinitarian doctrine. But he
considers it "neither particularly important nor interesting"
"whether Matthew actually teaches a doctrine of three in
one" (1985:158). While "a triune conception" of God's identity
is here said to be "grounded in a biblical narrative descrip-
tion" (ibid., 139), the conception of authoritative biblical
teaching is avoided and Chalcedonian Christology is not
expressly affirmed. It is rather solely "by grace" that our
human concepts and categories "are enabled to identify God
as Father, Son and Spirit" (ibid., 140), a formulation sufficiently
ambiguous to correlate trinitarian beliefs with personal
decision.

Leonardo Boff considers the Trinity not only a true statement about deity but a prototype also of just community
(which will transcend the conflict between capitalism and
socialism!). God is not a solitary One but a triunity of
co-eternal and co-related persons. Yet Boff combines this
with speculative notions that the Holy Spirit's presence
divinizes Mary and the whole creation.

Theological entrepreneurs seem to multiply who, while professing not to find in the New Testament a basis for classical credal affirmations, nonetheless profess to find there a legitimation of their own novel predilections. Maurice F. Wiles claims that the early church's worship of Christ confused the medium of divine revelation with the divine object of worship, God, and therefore fell into idolatry (1976: chap. 10). Wainwright responds that Athanasian Christology involved the contrary assumption: "The Church's worship of Christ was... the accepted fact, and the conclusion was drawn that since the worship of a creature would be intolerably idolatrous, the Son must be 'homousios' with the Father" (1980:18). Theologians like Wiles, moreover, distinguish *worship* of Christ from cognitive affirmations. But Wainwright rightly asks whether they can be trinitarian liturgists while they are intellectual unitarians? If Christ be not true God, is it not idolatrous to worship him as God? Is logical congruity dispensable between one's public liturgy and private cognition? (ibid., 181).

Yet Wainwright's own Christology is broadly kenotic (1980:205-10, 351-52). Wainwright stresses that Christ was confessed as Lord at baptism (1 Cor 12:3), invoked as Lord in Christian assembly (1 Cor 16:22), worshiped as Lord in anticipation of his final return (Phil 2:5-11), and prayed to for divine help in time of need (Acts 7:59; 2 Cor 12:8) (ibid., 47-48). Yet his notion that Christ embodied God's very character and being and lived the divine life of self-giving within the conditions of humanity need not require a pre-existent divine person's incarnation (ibid., 61). Wainwright thinks trinitarian doctrine may have arisen partly to meet the complaint that it is absurd that the living God, upon whom all life depends, should die, and he commends the controversial view that the Son suffered in his divine as well as human nature (ibid., 66, 210-11).

By the Trinity Pannenberg indicates the living God's particular and absolutely unique unity. He rests his trinitarianism on the historicality of God's revelation, in which the disclosure of God's being diverges into the Father, Son, and Spirit (1977:180). "If Father, Son, and Spirit are distinct but coordinate moments in the accomplishment of God's revelation,"

Pannenberg asserts, "then they are so in God's eternal essence as well" (ibid.). But does this follow necessarily? Pannenberg applauds Hegel, who may indeed have coordinated revelatory history with three divine persons existing for each other. But Pannenberg insists on their coexistence, leaping hurriedly—without adducing adequate epistemic supports—from a functional to an ontological Trinity. His attempt to conceptualize God's eternal essence from divine acts in history, exclusive of divine propositional revelation of the meaning of those acts or of the nature of transcendent reality, forfeits a sound basis for authentic metaphysical statements. In fact, Pannenberg considers the doctrine of the Trinity necessarily contradictory (ibid., 183), on the ground that we are but finite creatures coping with the infinite. But if our finitude renders metaphysical assertions logically contradictory, illogic haunts all that Pannenberg says about God, despite his appeal to revelatory history. In the end Pannenberg considers the Trinity merely doxologically significant, rather than an objectively conceptual entity.

Jurgen Moltmann's emphasis is no less confusing. Christian doctrine, he holds, must not be monotheistic but rather trinitarian. Worse yet, he does not clarify the truth-status of trinitarian claims. His conception of an "open Trinity" is speculatively panentheistic in bent (1981). He fails to supply warrants for the notion that God is ontologically open to and inclusive of man and the world. Moltmann writes: "The one person of Jesus Christ is not a matter of two metaphysically different 'natures.' It is an expression of his exclusive relationship to the Father, by reason of his origin, and his inclusive relationship of fellowship to his many brothers and sisters" (ibid., 120).

The volume by Pinchas Lapide and Moltmann titled *Jewish Monotheism and Christian Trinitarian Doctrine* (1981) may be doubly misleading. The title, for one thing, seems to imply that Christians are not necessarily monotheists. The content, moreover, suggests that Judaism and Christianity both affirm the everlasting threeness of God, whereas by this predication they now mean quite different things.

Paul K. Jewett (1975:4:271) emphasizes that the doctrine of the Trinity, which the great monotheistic religions of

Judaism and Islam reject "as a denial of the truth that God is one, really rests on the same foundation as the monotheism of the Old Testament." That foundation is irreducible to philosophical speculation, or to inferences from religious experience, or inferences even from divine redemptive events; it is rather God's self-disclosed being made known to inspired writers, usually in conjunction with redemptive historical acts.

Although Jewish nonbelievers deplored the high claims for Jesus as an unacceptable concession to polytheism, Christian believers in fact endured martyrdom rather than to worship the Roman emperor at the expense of "one God, the Father" and "one Lord Jesus Christ." Later Jewish rabbis conceded that Christians insisted on belief in one God, yet nonetheless affirmed that belief in the Trinity implies polytheism. Their attitude toward Moslems was notably more positive on the ground that Islam is not trinitarian.

Oscar Cullmann's monograph *Les Premieres Confessions de Foi Cretiennes* supports the claim that all the early Christian affirmations are christological in thrust. Although the trinitarian formula was developed subsequently to the Apostles' Creed, early faith in Christ did not exclude faith in the Father and the Spirit. The early affirmations are aspects of the single confession that Jesus is the Christ, and the whole gains its significance and content in relation to him.

Selections reflecting the christological debate that arose among Christians prior to the Council of Chalcedon have been gathered together by Richard A. Norris, Jr. (1980). Alongside conflicting views of Jesus fueled by ancient speculation, modern christological restatements often similarly seem to gain their motivation from contemporary metaphysical prejudices.

Discussion of Jesus as God

It is nothing less than remarkable that recent modern Christology tends to ignore discussion of Jesus as *theos*. Philip B. Payne, moreover, has identified many parables in which Jesus applies to himself figures—such as shepherd, king, rock, bridegroom, sower—that the Old Testament used typically of God (1981). To be sure, the term *theos* is regularly used of the Father, and skeptically oriented christologies are prone to view its less frequent references to Jesus as late ascriptions stimulated by Hellenic or Roman influences.

Charles M. Laymon (1971) thinks it "not likely" that the New Testament followers of Jesus "identified him fully with the being of God." He tells us that the application to the Son in Heb 1:8 of the reference "Thy throne, O God" (Ps 45:6) "should probably be thought of, not as equating Jesus with God, but as pointing to his uniqueness. Similarly, Paul's statement in Rom 9:5 sounds in the KJV as if he is calling Jesus "God," but the RSV has translated this differently so that it refers to the praising of God" (1971:1173a). Laymon will only say that Jesus' followers "regarded his relation to God as utterly unique, unshared by any other." But that is to say very little that is worth saying, for each of us has a private or unique relationship to God unshared by others.

Some relevant texts are no doubt debatable and a number may be set aside entirely. Among the latter, Murray J. Harris lists John 17:3; Gal 2:20; Col 2:2; 1 Thess 4:9; 1 Tim 1:17; 3:16; 5:21; Heb 3:4; Jas 1:1; and 2 Pet 1:2. Harris regards Matt 1:23 and Eph 5:5 as "highly improbable"; 1 John 5:20; 2 Thess 1:12; and Heb 1:9 he considers "improbable"; and Acts 20:28 only a "possible" application of *theos* to Jesus Christ. For all that, he finds John 1:18 and Romans 9:5 to be "probable"; 2 Peter 1:1; Heb 1:8; and Titus 2:13 to be "highly probable"; and John 1:1 and 20:28 to be certain.

The Johannine references are therefore crucial. They refer to Jesus in his preincarnate, incarnate, and post-resurrection states; and their import is ontological rather than merely functional. "In the christological use of *theos*," Harris comments, "we find both the basis and the zenith of New Testament Christology: the basis, because *theos* is one christological title that is primarily ontological in character and because the presupposition of the predominantly functional Christology of the New Testament is ontological Christology; the zenith, because *theos* is one christological title that explicitly and unequivocally asserts the deity of Jesus Christ" (lecture notes at Trinity Evangelical Divinity School, 1990).

Harris emphasizes that "even if the early church had never applied the title *theos* to Jesus, his deity would still be apparent in his being depicted as the object of human and angelic worship and of saving faith; the exerciser of exclusively divine functions such as creatorial agency, the forgiveness of sins, and the final judgment; the addressee in petitionary prayer; the possessor of all divine attributes; the bearer of numerous titles used of Yahweh in the Old Testament; and the co-author of divine blessing" (1980:271).

Small wonder, then, that Barth declares unhesitatingly: "This man is the Jehovah of the Old Testament, is the Creator, is God himself" (1949:85). Brunner comments that "When Jesus Christ...speaks to us as 'I'...God Himself is really speaking to us" (1950:227-28). The Fourth Gospel has at the outset the emphasis "the Word was God....No one has ever seen God; the only Son...has made him known" (1:1,18, RSV), and then leads on at the close to doubting Thomas's response to the Risen Jesus, "My Lord and my God" (John 20:28). The high Christology affirming both Jesus Christ's human life and his divine authority appears not only in the Fourth Gospel but, as J. L. M. Haire points out, is found in Paul's writings, and is "already implied by the writers of the Synoptic Gospels" (1965, p. 96).

Intelligibilty of the Incarnation

Much recent theological assault has questioned the intelligibility of the doctrine of divine incarnation. This confrontation has been fueled by "myth of God incarnate" literature which denies the doctrine's objective truth and by the neo-orthodox emphasis that the event is an illogical paradox that only faith can grasp. In *The Logic of God Incarnate* (1986) Thomas V. Morris replies to both these approaches in a new and spirited defense of two-nature Chalcedonian theology. Morris argues that "the best defense" of the orthodox Chalcedonian definition of the incarnation is "a good offense" (1989).

Although the attack on Chalcedonian Christology continues, the long theological preoccupation with "in-*carne*-tion" has recently yielded to new interest in the theme of "in-*psych*-ation." The basic affirmation of the Christian incarnation-doctrine, Morris emphasizes, is the identity statement that the second person of the Trinity is the same person as Jesus of Nazareth. Morris rejects kenotic Christology, the 19th century view that in the incarnation the divine Logos suspended all or some metaphysical attributes of deity. If Jesus Christ is divine, Morris insists, divine attributes are essential and were not set aside in the incarnation. If human properties are incompatible with divine properties, the consequences are costly for the emphasis that Christ Jesus has both divine and human natures.

Critics of the Chalcedonian formula argue that the incarnation-doctrine is illogical because divine being has properties that no human has and that humans have properties that no divine being may have. Contingency, replies Morris, is indeed a property common to all who are merely human. Yet it is not an essential human property. The humanity of Christ Jesus does not preclude his omniscience, omnipotence, omnipresence, and so on. Morris holds that as incarnate the one person Jesus Christ had two minds and ranges of consciousness, one canopying the other (ibid., 103). The two minds qualify the one person. The divine consciousness had full access to the human, but not the human to the divine, except as the divine mind now and then permitted. William Craig concedes that peccability—the predilection to sin—, e.g., is not essential to human nature; "the beatified are impeccable but human" (1987:493). Some theologians argue that sinfulness is a property of humanity, but Chalcedon expressly denies this of Christ. Yet Craig criticizes Morris's formulation on the ground that it projects the fantastic possibility—which Morris in fact does not affirm—of a humanity that is omnipotent and omniscient, whereas such properties attach to the one person through the divine nature alone. Craig opts instead for the Scholastic view that in the incarnation Jesus Christ was omnipresent and omniscient in his divine nature but not in his human nature.

The fact that individual beings now living are non-eternal and created, Morris insists, does not require that this necessity constitutes part of what it is to have a human nature. Some properties may be *common* to members of a natural kind, may even be *universal* to all members of that kind, without being *essential* to membership of the kind, Morris stresses (1986). An individual may be human "without being characterized by any of these limitation properties." If they characterize us, necessarily it will be "in virtue of the humans we are" and "not in our being human"(ibid., 102). A human nature involves "a human body and a human mind, no more no less" (ibid.). For God the Son to become human "he did not have to become a created, contingent being," Morris insists, but needed only to assume "a created, contingent body and mind of the right sort" (ibid.).

Morris proposes a "two-minds" view that does not require divinity's relinquishment of divine resources in assuming a human mind and body. "His taking on of a body and mind limited in knowledge, power and presence does not entail that he himself, in his deepest continuing mode of existence, was limited in knowledge, power or presence," he writes. God incarnate had at one and the same time "a limited human consciousness and an overriding divine mind." This involves "two distinct minds or systems of mentality...eternal mind...(and) distinctly earthly mind with its consciousness that came into existence and developed" (1986:149-51). These two minds stand in something like an asymmetric accessing relation. Everything present to the human mind of Christ was thereby present to the divine mind as well, but not vice versa. The human mind was active though limited, while the divine mind exercised omniscience. Morris suggests that the current psychological "multi-mind" view of persons according to which a person potentially has "a system of systems of mentality" offers somewhat of an analogy of metaphysical postulations distinctive of a two-minds person (ibid.).

What are the implications of the two-minds view for Christ's personal unity? Morris insists that the multi-mind theory is not incompatible with Christ's personal unity. In the case of a human mental system, one's mental system defines a person; to causally subsume or override that system abrogates personal freedom. But the definition of Jesus' person is not provided by a human mental system alone, since this was integrated also with a divine mind which at any stage of divine incarnation could have over-ridden or subsumed the human mental system without abrogating Jesus' freedom. Christian orthodoxy emphasizes that Jesus was fully human without being merely human. Morris insists that the kenotic theory is less plausible and less attractive than a two-minds alternative. In this ancient view which has been relatively neglected for a long time the Logos did not set aside omniscience in the incarnation, but rather combined two ranges of consciousness in an a-symmetric accessing relationship. The divine mind contained, but was not contained by, the earthly mind (1986).

In reply to the question how he avoids Nestorianism, Morris comments that insofar as the Nestorians did move toward or endorse a two-person view, they failed to understand the complexity compatible with unity of personhood. He thinks the current systems approach to understanding nature and personhood transcends that difficulty.

6

The Chalcedonian Definition

Therefore, following the holy Fathers, we all with one accord teach men to acknowledge one and the same Son, our Lord Jesus Christ, at once complete in Godhead and complete in manhood, truly God and truly man, consisting also of a reason able soul and body; of one substance [homoousios] with the Father as regards his Godhead; and at the same time of one substance with us as regards his manhood; like us in all respects, apart from sin; as regards his Godhead, begotten of the Father before the ages, but yet as regards his manhood begotten, for us men and for our salvation, of Mary the Virgin, the God-bearer [Theotokos]; one and the same Christ, Son, Lord, Only-begotten, recognized IN TWO NATURES, WITHOUT CONFUSION, WITHOUT CHANGE, WITHOUT DIVISION, WITHOUT SEPARATION; the distinction of natures being in no way an nulled by the union, but rather the characteristics of each nature being preserved and coming together to form one person and subsistence [hypostasis], not as parted or separated into two persons, but one and the same Son and Only-begotten God the Word, Lord Jesus Christ; even as the prophets from the earliest times spoke of him, and our Lord Jesus Christ himself taught us, and the creed of the Fathers has handed down to us.(The Definition of Chalcedon in *Documents of the Christian Church*, 2nd. ed, selected and edited by Henry Bettenson [New York: Oxford University Press, 1967], pp. 51-52)

The Chalcedonian Definition achieved fifteen centuries ago in A.D. 451 still remains very much at the center of the christological debate. For more than a century neo-Protestant and then more and more neo-Catholic theologians have aggressively questioned its formulation of two natures and one person. Already in the last century Hegel, Schleiermacher, and Ritschl contributed in distinct ways to the alternative doctrine of a unitary divine-human nature. Critics who reduced all theological doctrine to fallible reflection on religious experience have since Schleiermacher alleged that the Chalcedonian formula superimposed Greek metaphysics on Christianity, metamorphosed supposedly functional representations of Scripture into ontological claims, and contradicted more enlightened modern comprehensions of metaphysical realities. Bultmann, for example, rejected Chalcedon as presupposing supernatural realities outmoded by modern thought; in actuality, he contended, Chalcedon merely objectified an existential affirmation. Some modern theologians blame Chalcedonian Christology for modern unbelief, on the ground that—so he alleges—it shifted the object of devotion from God to man.

Craig A. Blaising traces the rejection of Chalcedonian commitments to four common complaints: "Logical incoherence, an abstract and metaphysical approach which ignores existential significance, a distortion of the biblical faith, and a Hellenizing of the Gospel" (1981:329). Writing on the Council's anniversary, Karl Rahner commented that the Chalcedonian Council concluded with the triumph of an ambiguous truth and left unanswered questions calling for deeper insights. Rahner, along with Edward Schillebeeckx and many others, seeks a modern restatement of what it means that Jesus Christ is "true God and true man."

C. Norman Kraus (1987:98) insists that the Nicene-Chalcedonian Christology lacks adequacy. Chalcedon abandoned "Immanuel language" for philosophical God-language, he claims, and in doing so "shifted the focus of theological meaning from its original New Testament intention" (ibid., 59, n.17). He contends that the prologue of John's Gospel was not intended to be interpreted in a "philosophical way" (ibid., 98-99). Kraus so dilutes the New Testament portrayal of Jesus that his reconstruction is tantamount to a vigorous rejection of it. In his view, Christ is not metaphysically the preexistent Son of God; the virgin birth and "miracle of incarnation" are not factual events but are poetry and allegory; Jesus' resurrection did not take place in public history (ibid., 77-79). To affirm Christ's divinity, Kraus contends, is to make a relational rather than an ontological statement (ibid., 103).

John Martin Creed (1930:132) declared the Chalcedonian Definition incoherent. In the same volume Nathaniel Micklem argued that "The Chalcedonian confession, formally and categorically, if not intentionally, contradicts both the Nicene confession and the surest religious intuition of the modern Christian" that Jesus is "most divine when most human" (1930:144).

Even otherwise broadly conservative and mediating theologians like Charles Gore (1922) and H. R. Mackintosh (1913) declared the Chalcedonian option unsatisfactory. John Knox, although emphasizing God's revelatory act in Jesus Christ, affirms nonetheless that the Chalcedonian statements about him are not to be considered "metaphysically accurate descriptions" (1958:26). D. M. Baillie considers "not unjust" the criticism that the Chalcedonian formula promotes "an unnatural dualism in the Christ whom we know from the Gospel story" (1948:152). He urges reinterpretation of the New Testament representations by "translating" them "into terms and categories that can communicate the living truth to modern men." Although Baillie criticizes kenosis theory that in the incarnation the Logos stripped himself of certain divine attributes, he does not illumine a specific Christological alternative (chap. 4).

A. N. S. Lane points out, however, that contextualization of the Gospel in Hellenistic society was simply part of the Church's task, even as Christian missions seeks to contextualize its message today. The use of Greek terms did not of itself preclude the expression of profoundly Christian truths (1982, p. 263). The Chalcedonian formulation, moreover, included emphases that fundamentally challenged Greek philosophical assumptions.

Alongside the modern tendency to declare key scriptural doctrines outdated and unbelievable, and to dismiss Nicea and Chalcedon as reflections of now outmoded biblical and Greek tenets, some critics affirm that Jesus is divine only in a functional or dynamic way.

John A. T. Robinson assesses Jesus' humanity through three modern representations—mythological, ontological, and functional—and considers the latter conceptuality the best present-day option. But Donald Guthrie questions whether the distinctions Robinson imposes retroactively are wholly appropriate to the first-century Christian appraisal of Jesus. Guthrie adduces extensive data from the New Testament to show that while Jesus' contemporaries nowhere doubted the reality of Jesus' humanity, they insisted nonetheless on the distinctiveness of his humanity as attested by his sinlessness and by the application of Christological titles to him, such as Suffering Servant and Logos (1981, pp. 238-338).

For Hans Kung also, the formula that Jesus Christ is "truly God and truly man" signifies only that Jesus is God functionally, not ontologically (1976:381-83). Edward Schillebeeckx (1979) strips the terms Son of God and pre-existence of ontological import and translates them into functional alternatives. Schillebeeckx holds that human experience supplies revelatory access to Christology, but he develops this theme obscurely. To be sure, we cannot glean from historical data alone that Jesus was and is the Christ. But when Schillebeeckx looks more especially to inner experience, he does not clarify how we are to discriminate such experience-claims from merely confessional or cultural affirmations. If Jesus is a figure "constructed out of the consciousness of twentieth century people," then, as David Wells (1984:170) puts it, Schillebeeckx has not assuredly moved beyond anthropology to Christology.

Earl Richard (1988) considers the New Testament view of Christ to be essentially functional rather than metaphysical and considers its Christological teaching to be basically an extension of an early account of Jesus' death and resurrection—a diffusion backward into preexistence and forward into heavenly ministry. One can readily understand why scholars skeptical of orthodox Christology are eager to reduce Pauline doctrine to a merely functional view and to regard the high view as a late construction. For as a matter of chronology the undisputed Pauline letters constitute the earliest Christian evidence by perhaps at least a decade; moreover, Paul was in direct and frequent contact with the early Christian leaders in Jerusalem and elsewhere, and may be presumed to reflect their view as well as his own.

R. H. Fuller grants that the New Testament does indeed frequently emphasize the functional aspects of Jesus Christ's divine ministry, yet that fact does not justify the verdict that it contains no ontological claims about Christ the Lord (1965:247-50).

In *Jesus: The Unanswered Questions* John Bowden asks whether the Chalcedonian Definition formulated by bishops meeting in the presently unfamiliar world of A.D. 451 "just across the water from what is now Istanbul" achieved finality when "in the conceptuality of Platonist philosophy" they explained how Jesus could simultaneously be both God and man (1988:72)? Or was it, he asks, a human construction "negotiated by fallible human beings against the background of the culture of their time as a result of particular developments (which could have been otherwise) and on the basis of particular presuppositions (which are open to critical examination)"? (ibid., 74). Was Chalcedon a "miraculously safeguarded absolute"? Was it required as a response to "utterly disastrous" alternatives? Or does it instead prevent the Christian church from comprehending the true humanity of Jesus?

Colin Gunton depicts the Christological conflict in terms of a division existing since Schleiermacher's time between those who believe the form of talk about Christ reflected by Nicea and Chalcedon and those who consider the old forms dispensable and would express the content in different forms. Others consider "the old forms indispensable in certain respects if the content is to be retained" (1983:51). Gunton insists that "it is very difficult to maintain a real continuity with earlier ages unless we can at least in some way affirm their words as our words" even if not used and understood precisely in the same way (ibid., 5). "In the last few centuries," he protests, "there has been a tendency to reject ontological Christologies on the ground that they are simply abstract theorizing, and it has become fashionable to reject the most technical of confessions, that of Chalcedon, as intellectually bankrupt." But, he comments, "views of its bankruptcy usually reflect a poor understanding of its historical place" (ibid., 168).

Much as the Chalcedonian Definition may by modern standards seem to be "lengthy, wordy and tortuous" and its language "couched in an obsolete philosophy," writes George Carey (1978:5), it encapsulates, nevertheless, the very core of Christianity and the church's continuing confession of Jesus as both human and divine. Brian Hefflethwaite (1987:4:25) rejects as baseless the notion that the Chalcedonian Definition is logically incoherent.

Oskar Skarsaune, the Norwegian Lutheran scholar, regards the Chalcedonian Definition "as reflecting great theological and ecclesiological wisdom" (1990:124). Aloys Grillmeier says that "the usual claim that the church at Chalcedan surrendered to Hellenistic formulas and abstract theology just is not valid. In any case, that was not the self-understanding or intention of the college of bishops at that time" (1975:285). Yet what we need to know is whether the Chalcedon Definition is merely an historical document or has permanent validity. Ontology and soteriology may and do mutually condition one another, but no satisfactory Christology can emerge if we insist only that Jesus of Nazareth be conceived as the presence of the eternal God in time and space, significant as that may be.

Dare we any longer believe in the divinity of Jesus precisely as Chalcedon understood it? John Ferguson comments that many in the pews no longer do so (1980:214). The decisively important issue, however, is whether this defection reflects the flawed guidance of contemporary theologians or whether the future of the church is at stake in a return to the New Testament and to Chalcedon.

Colin Gunton reminds us that "to say that the symbol of Chalcedon is couched in the conceptuality of its time—what other conceptuality could it have used?—is not to deny its candidature for truth, and in two senses: as an accurate summary of what the New Testament says about Jesus and as the truth about who Jesus is" (1990:231). To be sure, Gunton adds that this is not the final truth this side of eternity. He allows only revisable claims. But that is Gunton's own revisable prejudice.

If all beliefs are historically conditioned, as modern humanists maintain, even this grandiose speculative assumption has no more validity than any other. The notion that we can retain and affirm the historic formulas of faith by the device of dynamic equivalence plays fast and loose not only with the ancient doctrines but with the conception of truth as well.

Evangelicals and the Historic Formula

Whatever complaints there may be that Chalcedon did not fully or adequately grasp the riches of Christology, the fact remains that most evangelically orthodox, like traditional Catholic, theologians have shown little desire to undo the Chalcedon Definition.

Klaas Runia (1984) contrasts the Nicean and Chalcedonian statements about the person and natures of Jesus Christ, which all Christian churches accept in their official formularies, with inadequate variations proposed by Pannenberg, Schillenbeeckx, Küng, and others. Much as books like *The Myth of God Incarnate* (John Hick, ed., 1977) and Kung's *On Being a Christian* (1976) signal a defection from Chalcedon, such works as Aloys Grillmeier's *Christ in Christian Tradition*, vol. 1: From the Apostolic Age to Chalcedon (1957, rev. 1965) focus anew on the authority of apostolic teaching and the continuity between its witness and the Chalcedonian affirmation. Grillmeier makes the point that Chalcedon put Greek terminology in the service of the biblical teaching of divine incarnation and not the reverse (1965:555).

B. B. Warfield (1929:263) championed the Chalcedonian statement. John R. W. Stott (1985:34) approvingly quotes Warfield's view that Chalcedon brought together all the biblical data in a harmonious statement. Gordon H. Clark writes that

> The Christology of the New Testament is admirably summed up in the Creed of Chalcedon; and those who repudiate the creed... are simply not Christians. There may indeed be any number of people in the churches who have never heard of Chalcedon. There are undoubtedly some who have never heard of one person and two natures—a disgrace to the church they attend—but there is a great difference between being an ignorant Christian and being a witting repudiator of the doctrine (1979:65).

Gerald E. Bray contends that the Chalcedonian definition "is inclusive of every factor necessary to do justice to the

New Testament picture of Christ" (1978:3). Bray comments
that the Chalcedonian Council was confident that it stood "in
a tradition of exegesis going back to the apostles" and its
views can be supported still by an appeal to Scripture (1978:2).

Christopher Butler writes that "the Formula of Chalcedon...
makes a decisive—and in my view successful—effort to per-
ceive the intellectual respectability of Christianity.... The
real issue today is whether or not we *can* believe in Christianity.
Those who reject the Formula of Chalcedon are, almost
without exception, men who have in fact answered that
question for themselves in the negative" (1977:97, 99). John
Bowden is so confident of the formula's enduring role that he
comments that "the mainstream has rejected" whatever doctrines do not "match up to Chalcedon" (1988:225,n. 1).

Geoffrey W. Bromiley notes, however, that recent renewal
of interest in Chalcedon focuses less on metaphysical formulation than on doxological confession. Contemporary discussion therefore may not much advance philosophical concerns.
Yet current theologizing insists that "the humanity of Christ
is not a limiting factor which demands either a restriction or
a spasmodic and paradoxical manifestation of the divine
attributes, but a specific form in which the true and living
God can and does bring all His attributes to expression,
achieving a unity of person, a communion of natures, graces,
and operations, without any distortion of humanity on the
one side, or on the other any forfeiture of deity, whether
within the Godhead or in the human form" (1979:1:666).

Harold O. J. Brown concedes that the clearest vision of the
truth about the only Son of God and about his eternal being
in the tripersonal God was first attained in conciliar definition several centuries after the historical divine manifestation in the flesh of Jesus Christ. But he does not, on account
of the theological debate that called for Chalcedonian clarification, dispute either the decisive importance of the Gospel
sources or their depiction of the decisive role of Jesus Christ.
Whatever part politics played at Chalcedon, he emphasizes,
the council did not create Christology nor did it project a
view of Christ other than the Christ of the New Testament.
Brown comments that "there seems to be no way to deal with
the trinitarian and incarnational message of the New Testa-

ment without making use of the categories and concepts of
the Hellenistic civilization in which the New Testament was
proclaimed." He warns that contemporary calls for "de-
Hellenization and re-Semitization of Christianity... may be
at the expense of the doctrines of the Trinity and the incarnation" (1984:194).

H. Dermot McDonald says that "we can say more about
Christ than Chalcedon says, but we dare not say less" (1975:14).
Klaas Runia likewise remarks that we are "not allowed to
say less than Chalcedon" (1980:14). In *Encountering Jesus: A
Debate on Christology* (1988), Stephen T. Davis and Rebecca
D. Pentz argue for retention of classic Chalcedonian Christology,
against John Hick, John B. Cobb, Jr., and James M. Robinson.
The Chalcedonian Definition is reaffirmed also by the French
theologian Henri Blocher (1987).

Ramm argues for Chalcedonian Christology but considers
biographical data in the Gospels less than scientifically accurate and in the nature rather of fallible theological witness
and confession (1985:139). While he acknowledges that the
Gospels include "datable events," he considers the New Testament record about Jesus beyond harmonization. He ap-
proves Brunner's view that Christ is fully authoritative, but
Scripture only contingently and partly so, thus perpetuating
an unresolved dichotomy between the living and the written
Word.

Disavowal of Chalcedon

Yet the contributor of the essay on "Christology" in *The
Baker Encyclopedia of the Bible* (Walter A. Elwell, gen. ed.,
1988:1:439) declares the Chalcedonian doctrine incomprehensible. He protests that it "would seem to make the incarnate Son an ontological split personality" to say that "Christ
had 'two distinct intellects' and 'two distinct wills,' as some of
the fathers insisted."

The modern discussion in the main reviews the issues
already addressed at Chalcedon; it does not introduce factors
about the person of Jesus Christ that were unanticipated by
the Chalcedonian debate. Yet significant differences in the
relevant philosophical language serve easily to obscure some
basic matters. Despite Paul Tillich's rejection of the super-

natural and disavowal of the divinity of Jesus, even Tillich held that the Chalcedonian formulation correctly declares Christ to be fully God and fully man. Yet Tillich claims that "all attempts to solve the Christological problem in terms of the two-nature theory" have ended in "inescapable contradictions and absurdities" (1951-63:2:146). George Tavard properly deplores Tillich's Christology as heretical, since Tillich views Jesus Christ not as God become God-man, but rather as a man in whom God distinctly manifests himself (1962, p. 137).

One need not be surprised, therefore, by J. L. M. Haire's comment that some academics now defend Chalcedonian Christology "in ways which seem to endanger the very truths it stood for" (1956:95). Even an announced intention to remain faithful to Chalcedon provides no assurance of successful fulfillment of this objective.

Lionel S. Thornton assured us that while the two-nature doctrine was formulated at Chalcedon in defiance of current categories of thought, we have today quite different categories which do not suggest the old difficulties and which in certain respects definitely support the rationality of the Chalcedonian doctrine (1928). But Thornton's view that Christ's incarnation inaugurates a new and true human nature creates as many problems as it solves. For we can then now no longer relate human unregeneracy to a violated human heritage, or view Jesus as ongoingly the restorer of a forfeited humanity. And does this extension of divine incarnation in Christ then imply also that mankind is lifted potentially to divinity? Thornton's theory seems to compromise rather than to preserve the true sense of Chalcedon.

E. L. Mascall also obscures the distinction between the two natures when he identifies the *who* of Christ as the eternal Son and the *what* as qualitatively human (1943:69).

Wolfhart Pannenberg holds that the Chalcedonian doctrine that Jesus unites in himself two natures, divine and human, embraces an insoluble problem if one begins not with the historical man Jesus but with the insistence that in the one Christ these natures are "without confusion, without change, without division, and without separation." Post-Chalcedonian Christology, Pannenberg complains, expressed the unity of

Jesus of Nazareth with the Son of God in terms of the incarnation of the Logos in Jesus rather than in terms of a two-nature doctrine. To begin with divine incarnation, Pannenberg argues, is to doom to failure every effort to achieve a satisfactory Christology. A single person, Pannenberg contends, cannot participate in two completely different natures.

Pannenberg concedes that the ground of Jesus' abstract being was in the Logos, but he defines the term "person" relationally. He emphasizes that Jesus' unity with God was mediated through his unreserved dedication to the Father consummated on the cross and attested in resurrection. "The uniqueness of Jesus' humanity in his path of dedication to the Father has established the confession of Jesus as the Son of God" (1977:342). Jesus is simultaneously the revelation of God and the revelation of human nature and human destiny, which is to be raised to new life in eschatological union with God (ibid., 191-92). Although Jesus alone is identical with the eternal Son of God, the divine sonship mirrored as historical reality in Jesus' eschatological union with God may be shared by all who participate in Jesus' Sonship.

Pannenberg stresses God's "revelatorial presence" in Jesus. Hence the union of Jesus with God is initially understood as functional. "Until his resurrection, Jesus' unity with God was hidden" (1977:321). Only Jesus' personal community with the Father demonstrates that Jesus is the Son of God and the perception of that unity emerges solely from the perspective of his resurrection destiny (ibid., 283, 323).

Although Pannenberg holds Jesus' revelatory unity with the eternal God leads to the conceptual affirmation that Jesus is the pre-existent Son of God, he considers this preexistence mythical (ibid., 150-51). The unity of God and man in Jesus Christ attested by the resurrection ultimately identifies Jesus as the Son of God. Jesus' identity as the eternal Son of the eternal Father is given through his special relationship to the Father in the human historical aspect of his existence (ibid., 337).

The revelation of Jesus as the Son of God so identifies him with God's lordship that he is disclosed as eschatological ruler of all things, and hence also as their creative agent (ibid., 365). This creative mediation presupposed, Pannenberg says, an eschatological orientation that views the essence of things in terms of their goal or destiny, rather than in terms of beginnings (ibid., 396-97). It is through Jesus the Son that the Father establishes his Kingdom, and in this horizon of expectation the lordship of Jesus becomes fully apparent. "Everything is predestined toward Jesus, and he is predestined to the summation of the whole" (ibid., 381). John B. Cobb, Jr. calls for nothing less than a major revision of the meaning of Chalcedon. He would strip Jesus Christ of supernatural being and instead emphasize divine immanence in the human personality of Jesus. Yet he would nonetheless retain the emphasis on divine incarnation (1975:166). Thus to enmesh Christ in process and tentativity is, of course, not difficult if, as process-philosophy postulates, God himself is so enmeshed. Cobb mutes Christianity's once-for-all claims vis-a-vis nonchristian religions, while he argues from the Christian claim that the Logos is universally present to a view that heralds Jesus as divinity incarnate. Christ is, for Cobb, the power of "creative transformation" (ibid., 45).

The attachment of novel meanings to traditional terminology clouds much of contemporary discussion of incarnation doctrine. Cobb alerts readers to the fact that the nontheistic premises that govern Pannenberg's theology impart radical and novel implications to his rather orthodox language. "The resurrected Jesus is God proleptically," notes Cobb (1975:201). "The resurrection of Jesus establishes retroactively the deity of his earthly life.... He became essentially one with God in his resurrection, and only in the light of that consummation is it true that he was one with God in his entire life. That oneness is not to be conceived in terms of the co-presence of two substances but rather in terms of the final meaning and reality of the humanity as revealed in the resurrection" (ibid., 201).

"This man Jesus is not just man, but from the perspective of his resurrection from the dead...he is one with God and thus is himself God." So Pannenberg argues from Jesus' resurrection to his divinity (1977:323). Christianity's central Christological affirmation is thus suspended upon inferences from what can be judged reliable in the historical portrait of Jesus. The final goal of history is predisclosed in Jesus as the incarnation of the *eschaton*, the prolepsis of the End.

The prime difficulty with Pannenberg's discussion flows from his rejection of the supernatural and his adoption of the modern one-layer theory of reality. He approaches historical events through a cognitive exclusion of theistic supernaturalism. He considers God not presently extant. God lies in the future, not as a reality or being in addition to or beyond the world, but as the end itself. As Cobb comments, "God is what Jesus speaks of as the Kingdom of God."

Russell Pregeant too espouses a process hermeneutic to depict the Christ figure. He views Jesus not as the incarnation of a supernatural, personal, loving God, but as the full and definitive disclosure of a grace always and forever being given in the universe and issuing from its impersonal ground of reality (1978). Whatever else Jesus Christ may be for Pregeant, he is clearly not the eternal personal Son of God nor the once-for-all manifestation of divine redemptive *agape*.

Norman Pittenger as a process-theologian finds in Jesus a manifestation of God's universal activity and contends that "Jesus was different than men in degree" (1970:142). Pittenger insists that Jesus "did not think of himself as God" (ibid., 7). Reality is regarded as evolving to new and higher levels, and incarnation is viewed as the crown of God's continuing creative work. Christ emerges from humanity, and this emergence is the divine intent for all (cf. Alan Richardson, 1983:62). To restrict divine incarnation to Jesus of Nazareth, Pittenger contends, makes "the incarnation a docetic exception" (1970:81).

David Wells rightly emphasizes that a dipolar philosophy, which Pittenger and other process theologians espouse, dissolves a pure divinity and pure humanity, and merely circumvents the classical Christological issues (1984:162-63). Process-theory undermines the absolute uniqueness of Christ's person, for he is not considered to differ from others in kind but only in degree.

Some vocal hostility to the Chalcedonian formulation issues from social activists who in principle disavow theoretical exposition in order to promote praxis. The Roman Catholic scholar Jon Sobrino (1978), a revolution-oriented dogmatician writing in a Latin American context, shuns the Chalcedonian Definition and proposes that commitment to Jesus and consequent discipleship replace any abstract formulation. A

socially-oriented decision-theology affirms Jesus to be Lord
in the church while it considers Marx lord over world history.
This now discredited approach often associates spiritual paci-
fication with Christ and political liberation with Marx.

The recurring appeal to regnant modern philosophy as
sufficient reason for abandoning incompatible views rests on
a presumptive culture-pride more than on truth. Modern
philosophy is not necessarily superior to ancient philosophy;
at its best it even sometimes echoes enduring aspects of
ancient philosophy. Nor has "modern philosophy" achieved a
consensus. Nor is it necessarily superior to the philosophy of
the future; the philosophy of the end-time will prevail over it.
The fifth-century church proclaimed the gospel in its contemporary situation, and the Chalcedonian Definition attempted
faithfully to credalize the New Testament witness.

Limitations and Reservations

A. N. S. Lane points out that in numerous respects it was
more difficult philosophically for the contemporaries of early
Christianity to accept the doctrine of divine incarnation than
it is for moderns. Such notions as God does not love the world
and matter is evil were deeply ingrained in classic Greek
speculation.

Harold O. J. Brown says that since Chalcedon the history
of doctrine has made "no substantial additional progress"
beyond the goal and limits of Christological teaching. "Renewed
attempts, such as the kenotic Christology of the nineteenth
century or the secular Christology of recent years, must be
seen as regressions rather than as progress" (1984:193).

Yet William Searle, Jr., thinks that the classic formulas
hammered out at Nicea and Chalcedon, although "accurate
and necessary in their place," nonetheless "are defensive
formulas which do little to anchor Christian doctrine in its
Hebrew origins" (1989:19). Yet Syriac Christology makes
much the same claims for Jesus Christ as does Chalcedonian.
The contrast of Greek (or Syriac) with Hebrew categories
and concepts should therefore not be overstated.

A. N. S. Lane takes a qualified approach. Chalcedon, he
claims, is valuable for its exclusion of such heresies as
Arianism, Apollinarianism, Nestorianism, and Eutychianism,

against which it proclaims "a positive Christology" (1982: 273-74). He declares Chalcedon a fifth-century "culturally relative" document that needs retranslation into contemporary terms; Chalcedonian Christology is flawed, he thinks, through "the intrusion of the unbiblical belief in an immutable and impassable God" (ibid., 274). But he thinks a correction of Chalcedon "is likely to come through a modification of Chalcedon, building on the achievement of Chalcedon, rather than an attempt to start again from scratch" (ibid.). Yet since Lane declares even the concepts of the Bible to be "culturally relative," it is difficult to see why a contrast of biblical with unbiblical beliefs could be decisive (ibid.). The notion that the transcendent God of the Bible—except for his moral nature and purposes—is mutable and vulnerable to suffering needs much more convincing support and, if true, has more serious theological consequences than Lane discerns.

Klass Runia comments that Barth fully accepted the Chalcedonian formulation of Christ's two natures and rejected as rationalistic speculation the modernistic disavowals by Herder and Harnack (1982:300). Barth took Chalcedonian Christology as a departure point to engage in the post-Chalcedonian debate. Barth stressed the full deity and full humanity of Jesus Christ; all divine attributes were present in the incarnation, as was a full human nature. He insisted that Christ is ontologically God, not merely functionally so. To emphasize Logos in the flesh he predicates of God both the names Jesus of Nazareth and Jesus Christ. Although he uses the name Jesus of the eternal Son, he does not hold that the divine attributes are communicated to and exercised by Christ's human nature.

Yet Barth goes beyond the insistence that the incarnation is the locale of God's revelation and that the supreme revelation is given in Jesus of Nazareth. In violation of traditional orthodoxy, he declares that the divine participates in the human and channels both humanity and becoming into the Godhead. Barth seems at times to confuse divine and human natures, as when he affirms that God is the subject of Jesus' suffering on Golgotha. Moreover, Barth is reluctant to affirm unambiguously the historical incarnation and resurrection. He locates these divine acts in the supposed realm of *Geschichte*, a divine-human relationship which, as Richard A. Muller comments, "seems to draw the Christ-event so into the Godhead that it cannot be in any sense an event in our history" (1986:133).

David Wells (1984) selects Barth, Pittenger, and Schillebeeckx to illustrate the divergence and confusion characteristic of recent twentieth-century Christology. The divergence results, at bottom, from a questioning of normativity of the Scripture and a tendency to locate theological meaning in the interpreter rather than in the text; from the vain search for a nonsupernatural historical Jesus behind the Gospels; and from fluid contemporary notions of God's identity and nature. Wells insists that "some form of the enhypostatic union must be employed if justice is to be done to the full range of New Testament teaching" (ibid., 177). "The person of the God-man is the person of God" and not a "hybrid union," while yet the humanity of Jesus is complete (ibid., 179).

Chalcedon and the Person of Jesus

The Christology of Athanasius has in recent years been gaining attention by scholars who suspect, rightly or wrongly, that it may have bequeathed to Chalcedon problems that shaped what many moderns consider a wrong response. In brief, Athanasius is declared to be the sponsor of a view of human divinization that escalated into a belief in Christ's deity (cf. M. F. Wiles, (1967:107-08); moreover he is labeled also as the proponent of a "soul-less" human nature in Christ (cf. W. Pannenberg, 1977:49). But, as Roy Kearsley contends in an unpublished paper ("Athanasius: Christological Culprit?"), Athanasius's insistence on Christ's deity involved much more than a relationship between deity and deification. Athanasius was not, moreover, entirely locked up to a denial of Jesus' true humanity, so it would be "inappropriate to describe Athanasian Christology as a proto-anhypostasia," i.e., as involving a denial of Christ's human person. Although leaning in places toward an Apollinarian denial that Jesus had a fully human mind, Athanasius did not hold a kenotic view that limits Christ's power and knowledge to his human mind and body during the incarnation.

Gordon Clark considers the absence of definitions a fatal

flaw in the Chalcedonian creed (1988:15). Terminological inconsistency and confusion, he protests, underlie the historic Christian doctrinal emphasis that Jesus Christ was "a divine person and in no way a human person" (ibid., 53). The Chalcedonian Definition, as Robert Crawford comments, "has always raised the objection, apart from its credibility, that it makes 'impersonal' the humanity of the man Jesus since it is taken up into the eternal identity of the Logos or Son" (1985:83). Although Clark is no foe of credal Christianity, he nonetheless complains that while in respect to unintelligible wording and undefined terminology "the Nicene Creed is not so bad; the Creed of Chalcedon's negative statements are passable; but from then on, including the Athanasian Creed, unintelligibility and meaningless expressions have characterized the discussions" (1981:51). "Even Augustine's *De Trinitate* could be improved here and there," he adds (ibid).

The Chalcedonian creed, Clark emphasizes, speaks of Jesus Christ as being both "truly God and truly man," indeed of "*a reasonable soul* and body." Clark translates *psyches logikes* as "rational soul." That Jesus had a human soul, he adds, is clear from the Gospels (e.g., "My soul is exceedingly sorrowful even unto death," Matt 26:38; Mark 14:34; cf. also John 12:27; Acts 2:27 quoting Ps. 16:8-11). But Clark criticizes Charles Hodge's exposition of this "rational soul" as a "finite human intelligence . . . a perfect and complete human nature" that "entered into the composition of Christ's person." For, Clark stresses, "Christ's person was deity . . . eternal and immutable," and his human nature in no sense composed his person (ibid., 42-43). Clark also criticizes W. G. T. Shedd's exposition. Shedd denies that the Trinity was altered by the incarnation, yet confusingly says also that "the God-man was a new person." At the same time Shedd denies that the man Jesus was a person, although saying that Mary was the mother both of Jesus' human soul and human body. Clark stresses that Jesus not only was a (human) nature, but was nothing less than "a man" (1988:50).

Clark contends that we should "completely banish from theology" the term "substance" and as the price of retaining the term "person" should insist on clear definition (ibid., 52). The meaning of the word "person", he stresses, is horrendously confused even in our day. Multitudes deny that unborn babies are persons. Athanasius had already emphasized that "the substance of God" was merely another way of referring to God and does not imply an underlying element to which attributes or perfections are superadded (cf. C. F. H. Henry, 1979:5:119).

But if we may advantageously discard the term "substance," not so the term "person," affirms Clark, though it needs more precise definition. To argue, as have many theologians, that Jesus is not a "person" is in effect, Clark insists, to deny that he was "a man" and to make him only "a nature" or "act of qualities attaching to the Second Person" (1988:77). But that "attaches contradictory characteristics to a single Person" and, equally objectionable, attaches to deity "the characteristics of an ordinary man."

Karl Barth, it may be recalled, also held that Christ's human nature included what we call personality for it had no being by itself. That the subject who utters the "I" when Jesus speaks is human has been held by Jesuit Paul Galtier (1939:237-371), who insists on the personal unity of Christ and the full autonomy of the human nature. Ralph J. Tapia comments that "A Christ who is presented as endowed with a fully human psychological personality is certain to make a greater appeal to an age that is profoundly interested in problems of psychology" (1971:449).

Clark ventures to define person "as a composite of truths... or a bit more exactly... a composite of propositions" (1988:54). "A person is the propositions he thinks" (ibid., 55). Scripture itself affirms that God is truth, that there is no truth except that which constitutes the mind of God. But does this view—that a person is the propositions he thinks—Clark asks rhetorically, then reduce the Godhead to "one Person"? Emphatically not, he responds. Though the three persons are omniscient, they do not all know, i.e., experience, the same truths: The Father cannot say "I walked from Jerusalem to Jericho"; only the Son can say "I was incarnated"; and the Spirit cannot say "I begot the Son." In short "each of the three persons is omniscient without having precisely the same content" and hence each is distinctive (ibid.).

The incarnation did not deprive the incarnate Son of his

divine attributes; he was and remains a divine person. Yet we must not declare the human nature "impersonal," Clark insists (ibid., 69), since (to quote A. A. Hodge) Jesus Christ as God-man possessed "in the unity of His person two spirits with all their essential attributes, a human consciousness, mind, heart, and will." To reinforce his point, Clark asks, "If the [divine] person, being the Logos, could not be crucified, was our salvation accomplished by the death of an impersonal nature?" The verses Matt 27:46 and Mark 15:34 ("My God, my God, why hast thou forsaken me?") surely do not refer to a rift within the Trinity, Clark stresses, but presuppose God's forsaking not merely of a "nature" but of a person (ibid., 70-71). The unhesitating New Testament emphasis on Jesus Christ as "a man" (cf. John 8:40; Acts 2:22; 1 Tim 2:5) points in the same direction.

Yet Clark concedes that the relationship of the divine and human personhood is not easily resolved. "It is difficult to believe that the divine knowledge of the incarnate Son had no effect on or relationship to the human knowledge of Jesus; but it is equally difficult to decide what that relationship was" (ibid., 72).

Here one recalls the comment of Tertullian (*Against Praxeus*, 30) that Jesus' cry on the cross was not the voice of God or of the Word of Spirit, but rather of the flesh, the soul, the voice of a human being. Oskar Skarsaune comments that a distinguishing feature of that western Christology as it followed in Tertullian's path was its reference to the two natures "almost as independently acting subjects" (1991:97). Skarsaune notes that even the Alexandrians, to whom such views were an abomination, "drew back from acknowledging in too direct a manner the Logos' limitations and suffering. Even Athanasius drew back," he adds, "from lodging Jesus' human psychology in his Logos-ego; he placed it in the flesh (*sarx*)" (ibid., 108). A century later Cyril of Alexandria, who became beside Athanasius the classical exponent of Christology, modified the Alexandrian view by writing of "the soul of Jesus." The Cappadocians, and then Cyril, also allowed a larger role for Jesus' *psyche*, arguing from humanity's need for the redemption of the whole self to the assumption by Christ of all that belongs to human-ness. Theodore of Mopsuestia criticized

Arius's disciples for saying that "Christ took on a body but not a soul; the divine nature, they say, takes the place of the soul" [cited in Grillmeier, (1965:344-45)]. The soul is our life-principle, limited to be sure, since humans suffer; Jesus, who shared the human limitations, had a human soul as an aspect of his complete humanity. It would be docetic to contend that the Logos completely absorbs the human nature except for the flesh. Since it is the soul that sins, a redemptive death presupposes that Christ assumed a soul and a body on account of the soul.

Critics charged that this divided Jesus Christ into a self-sufficient human with a merely indwelling Logos; they felt he had not clearly amalgamated the Logos-ego and the human-ego in terms of one person and threatened the one "I" or one subject. Theodore thus contributed to the accelerating demand for Chalcedon and its great precision. Specialists in the history of doctrine have more and more held that Theodore's disciple, Nestorius, has been unfairly charged with heresy in his conflict with Cyril of Alexandria, who emphasized personal-subject unity in Christ while viewing Jesus as an active subject. Nestorius meanwhile stressed the true and complete humanity of the God-man.

The Council of Ephesus (A.D. 431) marked the rout of Nestorianism (which held that Jesus was a human person) and the victory of the Christology represented by Cyril of Alexandria. Cyril declared the same person or subject to be both the eternal Son of God and the son of Mary, so that the Creator assumed the mortal conditions of humanity, including death, on the way to the divine eternity. Some of Cyril's successors—Eutyches among them—spoke of Christ's humanity as "deified" from the moment of conception, in which case his humanity could hardly be regarded as consubstantial with ours. Churchmen consequently were constrained to repudiate the Eutychian heresy of "monophysitism"—or that Jesus Christ had but one nature. Others insisted that the absence of a human hypostasis ("person") in Jesus need not imply that his manhood ceases to be an existential reality (cf. John Meyendorff, 1975:79).

The Chalcedonian Definition (A.D. 451), Meyendorff insists, was never intended as a new creed for liturgical, sacramental or "symbolic" use, but rather was "a statement excluding both the Nestorian and the Eutychian heresies" (ibid., 177). In the Eastern Orthodox churches three trends emerged in the subsequent interpretation of Chalcedon (ibid., 216.; cf. also P. T. R. Gray, 1979:451-553), and theological clarification become necessary if there was to be universal acceptance.

The Chalcedonian Definition, it developed, engendered the first major and lasting division in Eastern Christendom. To this day the Syrian Jacobites, Copts, and Armenians (so-called Monophysites) have refused to accept its conclusions (cf. *Greek Orthodox Theological Review*, 10:2 [1964-65]; W. H. C. Frend, 1972). Because of widespread terminological confusion that involved an interchangeable use of "nature" and "person," the so-called Monophysite understanding of Chalcedon—which spoke of Christ existing in the inseparable unity of "two natures" forming "one person and one subsistence" —involved a fear of Nestorianism and a kind of Cyrillian extremism.

Chalcedon had indeed insisted that Christ is one in his personal identity but, as Meyendorff says, "it did not clearly specify that the term hypostasis, used to designate this identify, also designated the hypostasis of the pre-existing Logos" (1979:153). This is why Chalcedonian Christology subsequently had to refine its use of the term *hypostasis*. Leontius of Jerusalem ventured a more precise interpretation. He argued that Christ's human nature (*physis*) did not exist impersonally (*an*hypostatically) but personally (*en*hypostatically) in the preexisting and eternal person of the divine Logos. In Jesus Christ, therefore, there are not two persons but one. This position was proclaimed Orthodox at the Fifth Ecumenical Council in 553 which also pledged loyalty to Chalcedon and Cyril of Alexandria. Meyendorff explains that the term *hypostasis* "implied a peculiar double character of the specifically *personal* existence—continuous *identity* and openness to *existential change*" (1987:13). The incarnation, therefore, implies in this view that the Logos willingly underwent change whereas the divine nature (*ousia*, *physis*) remained immutable. The *en*hypostasizing of human nature by the divine Logos affirms that the *Word* suffered *humanly*. Since believers are *in* the person of Christ *our* personhood can be deified.

Any theological redefinition of personhood has important theological consequences for both Christian-Muslim and for Christian-Jewish dialogue. The Koran simply does not come to terms with Jesus, although it concedes that he was born of the virgin Mary by a miraculous act of Allah (Sura 3:47) and grants his miracle-working powers. It strips the gospel from Jesus' lips, however, and implies that his ascension occurred without death and resurrection (Sura 4:157). Along with the doctrine of the Trinity, it deletes the doctrine of divine incarnation in Jesus. The Koran caricatures the doctrine of the Trinity as belief in three separate gods in intimate partnership, rather than understanding it as one God subsisting in three persons (Sura 112). Because Muslims insist on using the terms *Shakhsun* for *persons* and refer it to disparate and discrete individuals only, the Christian insistence on three persons is made to imply three co-existing gods. To avoid this confusion and to refocus the issue some scholars, among them Gleason L. Archer (unpublished paper), contend that the term *hypostasis* may be preferable to *persona* in Christian-Muslim dialogue. The Eastern Orthodox formulation, following Chalcedon, speaks of a hypostatic union of divine and human natures in the incarnation and of three *hypostases* in one Godhead.

Gordon Clark's final illness interrupted completion of his manuscript on the incarnation and expansion of his previously quoted comment on Chalcedon. Surely Jesus was born as a person and suffered as a person. But Clark's insistence that "Jesus Christ was and is both God and man, a divine person and a human person," sets the discussion of Chalcedon in new focus. To say that Christ became God-man requires us to affirm, he insists, that he is divine person and human person; to deny either is to imperil either his deity or humanity.

Clark comments briefly and only in passing on the Nestorian heresy (1988:75). Those who charge Nestorius with holding that "the incarnation resulted in two persons" misinterpret him, he thinks, and do so for two reasons. For one, they likely confuse Nestorius's views with those of some of his followers; for another, neither Nestorius nor his opponents "had any clear idea of what a *person* is" any more than many others did of the term *substance*, or for that matter, the term *nature*. Shall we then press the distinction of two natures into one of double personality? Clark seems to avow what was only implicit in Nestorian theory, two natures with personal independence. But Clark speaks also of a duality of persons in Christ, yet does so only in the context of a highly specific definition of person.

Morris regards Clark's view that a person is a collection of propositions "more than exceedingly odd," on the ground that propositions are most often understood as abstract objects, but persons as paradigmatic of concrete objects. Yet Clark leans toward a personalistic rather than a Thomistic view and avoids a distinction between substance and attributes. Moreover, he sees propositions in terms of a living mind and not in terms merely of abstract or static phenomena.

Yet personality would seem to include both mind and will. If will is coordinated with nature rather than with person, the implication would seem to be that there is but one will in the triune Godhead.

J. S. Lawton commented a generation ago that "If higher criticism had been purely a matter of impartial science, then in the long-run the findings of scholars at Oxford and at Tubingen should have been in substantial agreement. The fact that they were not leads, in the end, to the conclusion that the *a priori* method had been abandoned by neither side" (1943:7-8). English scholars opted for divine *kenosis*, which German scholars had already abandoned. But they shared a mutual hostility to Chalcedonian theology, and as a necessity for understanding Jesus Christ's psychic experience from our side, rejected two centers of consciousness. Both agreed that Jesus did not posses divine attributes as such (a single instance like Mark 13:32 was taken as sufficient to overthrow omniscience), yet that he is to be distinguished from mankind generally in some superlative sense. If "kenoticists" meant by this that the deity is on the divine side, the German scholars, consistently enough, were unready to identify as divine what was declared to be "depotentiated" and "reduced."

Beyond Chalcedon

Discussion of Christology now may be on the threshold of an exciting new epoch involving Protestant evangelical and Eastern Orthodox theologians, and possibly Roman Catholic scholars as well. One leading Orthodox spokesman insists, as we have noted, that his communion has never considered Chalcedon the last word, and that its ambiguities must be addressed if we are to avoid theological confusion. One of evangelical Protestantism's most distinguished philosophers stresses that the precise definition of personhood remains an unfinished task, offers a new option, and insists that biblically-controlled Christians must affirm both the divine and human personhood of Jesus Christ. Another competent conservative philosopher emphasizes that a two-mind theory best accounts for the New Testament representations of Jesus Christ; this explanation, he contends, preserves the intentions of Chalcedon and avoids the defects of subevangelical and nonevangelical views. The stage seems set, therefore, for an acceleration of theological discussion over the God-man of Galilee.

"Many histories of the development of Christology end with the Council of Chalcedon. The impression is thereby given that Chalcedon marks a sort of closure, the 'last word' about Christ in the Early Church's theological development. That is certainly not the case." So comments Oskar Skarsaune. "One could rather say just the opposite: Chalcedon *opened up* the greatest Christological struggle in the Eastern church.... The lack of unanimity regarding the Chalcedonian Definition led to permanent church schism in the Eastern Church." (1991:126). "Chalcedon can just as well be considered," writes Skarsaune, "the prelude to a new phase in the Christological controversy as the conclusion of an earlier one" (ibid., 129).

Christian orthodoxy will probe with new interest the implications of the church's historical insistence on the full deity and full humanity of Jesus Christ, and on the unity of his personality in opposition to a dual life with two unintegrated centers of motivation. Assuming that these historic doctrinal affirmations are not to be undone, they will earnestly debate the question whether personal unity is jeopardized by the widening contemporary insistence that divine incarnation in

Jesus Christ involved two sets of conscious processes, or as some would prefer to say, two persons (provided we do not take for granted the definition of personhood). What underlies much of the reluctance to probe such questions is the widespread modern assumption, nurtured by so-called scientific-historical criticism, that Jesus Christ's "personality" *must* be understood in terms of a psychological unity essentially identical with that of other persons and through categories derived from general psychology. Modern theology assumed that affirmation of a dual consciousness would make historic study of Christ impossible and would destroy any unity of consciousness. But Christian orthodoxy has been convinced that two centers of knowledge and action in Jesus Christ need not mean dual personality, any more than three persons in the Godhead mean tritheism. No less than the church of the first and sixth centuries, the church today has the New Testament records, and it is from biblical theology, and not from modern philosophy or psychology, that decisive verification alone can come.

Conclusion:

Anticipating an Era of Christological Vigor

The French social philosopher Jean Milet (1981:45-46) sternly critiques what he calls "excesses of Christocentricity" in recent Christian thought and practice. The term christocentrism carries a variety of meanings, and not all who affirm or resist it have in mind the same thing.

Eugene TeSelle, for example, opposes its frequent implication that Christ's incarnation is central to God's creation and to all divine activity in the world (1975:xi). The ground of his rejection is significant. TeSelle entertains an evolutionary view which denies that God's purposes are fully defined from eternity; instead, he postulates a cosmic development "from indeterminacy toward definiteness" (ibid., 163).

Milet's disapproval of christocentrism, by contrast, has in view something quite different. As a social pyschologist he analyzes significant tensions between theocentric and christocentric elements especially in his own Roman Catholic communion. Catholicism was mainly theocentric from the fourth to the seventeenth century, he stresses, but thereafter christocentric emphases escalated until christocentricity now largely preempts the field. Milet finds unwarranted christocentricity in emphases such as that Christian truth is "not a principle but a man"; or that Christians are related to a God of love but not to a God of justice or of transcendent omnipotence or of immutability; or that Christian experience turns all divine imperatives into an inner invitation to do right.

One might add also the emphasis on stigmata in depicting the believer's participation in the sufferings of Christ; fanciful misuse of the biblical doctrine that believers are the bride of Christ; dialectical notions that Christians must live a life of intellectual paradox; the deterioration of prayer into a

115

rambling "dear Jesus" monologue; the readiness of Jesus-people to substitute "a cheer for Jesus" for recital of the Apostles' Creed; and not least of all the transubstantiation claimed for the Roman mass.

Milet makes the point that "Christ himself is theocentric (and not christocentric)":

> all his thoughts and actions are directed to the glory of God, the worship of the 'Father which is in heaven'.... The Christ never presents himself as coming to inaugurate a new religion of which he will be the centre, and where the worship of God will be attenuated for his benefit.... What the first Christians saw in Christ was not the principle of a new religion; it was rather the occasion willed by God for renewing traditional religious life (1981:77).

Yet for all that, Jesus no doubt signalled *fulfillment* and not mere amendment of the Hebrew heritage. The "I am," "I am come," and "But I say to you" passages lift Jesus above the prophets ontologically as well as epistemologically. The Johannine Logos references declare that Jesus Christ is the incarnation of divine personhood. Paul depicts Jesus not only as the one mediator but as essentially the revelation of God as well. The major development in the expanding Pauline christology, Milet contends, was no longer the Spirit's coming but the coming of Christ; in Milet's words, "Easter gradually 'dethroned' Pentecost" (1981:78). To Paul the apostle, Milet traces a worship and adoration of Christ that fourth and fifth century conciliar definitions only render more precise.

The New Testament nonetheless compels us to concede, Milet cautions, that the faith of the early Christians did not cease to be theocentric. This theocentric orientation remains largely predominant among the church fathers of the second, third, and fourth centuries, he adds (1981:80), despite "a slight trend" toward christocentricity among the Latin fathers. Christological worship did not involve a clear recentering of faith on Christ instead of God. The two emphases are held in theoretical equilibrium.

Yet in practice a strictly christocentric worship slowly arises, leading to christocentric hymns and readings, and in time to the Roman mass. Whereas in Eastern Christianity theocentricity prevails, in Western Christianity it endures only until the Renaissance, when the rise of humanism gives man—not God—center stage.

Milet has an evident distaste for the Protestant Reformation. While he concedes the Reformers' theocentricity, he claims that the attention Reformation churches devoted to the Bible encouraged an objectionable christocentricity. Because the New Testament focuses largely on Christ's historic person, Milet suggests, the availability of Scripture probably led logically "to nineteenth century liberal Protestantism and the christocentricity which it defends" (1981:107). One would think that an exaggerated or defective christocentrism would rise instead from a failure to give proper heed to Scripture with its carefully balanced theocentric and christocentric content.

The supposed tension between theocentricity and christocentricity is distorted by those who think Paul fundamentally modified the religion of Jesus by twisting His emphasis on imitation of God—identified as the historic view of Judaism—into a christocentrism that inserts an intermediary "between the imitator and his ultimate divine model." So contends Geza Vermes (1987:149). As Vermes sees it, Paul's exhortation "Be imitators of me as I am of Christ" (1 Cor 11:1) "originated the trend still conspicuous in the more ancient forms of Christianity, to multiply mediators and intercessors between the faithful and God: Jesus, Paul, Mary the mother of Jesus, the martyrs, the saints. But against this notion we must range Paul's insistent witness: "There is one mediator between God and man, the man Christ Jesus" (1 Tim 2:5). To argue as Vermes does that "the religiosity of primitive Christianity became trained on the mediator in place of God"—so that christocentricity displaces theocentricity—is a profound misunderstanding, one that no careful study of the New Testament worship will substantiate.

Milet traces the modern radical Catholic drift toward atheistic Christianity—'Christianity without God'—to the so-called "French school of spirituality," a seventeenth century doctrinal and spiritual phenomenon. The formative influences were Cardinal P. de Berulle and his disciples, who distanced themselves from scholastic theocentrism and in the context of the Renaissance sought "to show that the Christian is as humanist"

as other persons, and that "Christianity is itself a humanism" (1981:113). Their motif became that "Jesus Christ was
the most human of men"—indeed was the first humanist—
and that the God-man should be revered as man.

Alongside this development confidence in philosophical
reasoning and conceptual analysis declined, an emphasis
arose on historical knowledge of Christ rather than on cognitive knowledge of the transcendent God as the source of
spiritual certainty, and interest deepened in experiment and
experience. Instead of proceeding from God to Christ, the
new approach looked first to Christ through the Gospels;
beyond that, any arrival at God became increasingly problematical. What rendered this view extravagantly christocentric
was its emphasis that "belief in Christ forms the centre of
the religious life and belief in God is as it were extra for the
believer" (Milet, 1981:116). Only in the incarnate Word is
the incomprehensible, ineffable, and invisible God known
and heard and seen; the object of all religious knowledge and
spiritual obedience is Jesus only. Christ thus replaces God as
the center of Christian faith and activity.

Milet gives an historical overview of the consequences of
this approach. Initially, in view of human awareness of God
as the primal being, it did not exclude a supplementary
theocentric stage. Yet the center of world history was now
found in the historical event of divine incarnation. God was
no longer discerned through the cosmos, conscience, and
human nature; divine incarnation and faith in Jesus Christ
became decisive for knowledge of God.

Yet Berullian christocentricity never entirely displaced
theocentricity. Both the Orthodox church and the Reformation churches escaped its impact. Many theologians refused
to confine their interest solely to God's historical manifestation and contemplated God as a theoretical entity. Except for
Malebranche (1638-1715), philosophical and scientific thought
in the seventeenth and eighteenth centuries was theocentric.

But in the seventeenth and eighteenth centuries, Milet
avers, christocentrism notably penetrated institutional Catholic social structures, liturgical life, and spiritual practices.
It altered even the Catholic conception of the priesthood,
viewing it more basically as a presence of Christ among

humans than as a clerical representation of humans to God (1981:132-33). In the nineteenth century, belief in the existence of the transcendent invisible God began to crumble, although it had been held even in ancient times by Jews and then by Greeks and Romans (whether Christian or nonchristian) and subsequently prevailed throughout the Middle Ages. Modern naturalism first nurtured the rise of a mild atheism among an intellectual elite, and then also among the populace. Belief that "a god who ordered the world" was the "common metaphysical basis of human consciousness" was now questioned (ibid., 139). Hegelian pantheism was a nostalgic but unsuccessful effort to recapture a theocentric basis, as were other attempts that spoke of a god not really God. The more radical negations of Feuerbach and Marx and Freud strove to strip theocentricity of all valid objective content.

As an alternative to philosophical argumentation, Catholic scholars in the first third of the twentieth century, notes Milet, turned for the vindication of theism to historical divine revelation, and pursued biblical exegetical work. So-called positive theology rediscovered "the God of Jesus Christ." The new preoccupation with the Apostles' Creed could be summed up in the one emphasis: "Jesus Christ": God's "only Son our Lord, conceived by the Holy Ghost, born of the virgin Mary, suffered under Pontius Pilate, was crucified, died and buried. He descended into hell. The third day he rose again, and sitteth at the right hand of God the Father almighty."

Meanwhile, Protestant liberalism's reconstruction of christology from Harnack onward, coupled with a bureaucratic longing to update denominational creeds, reflected more interest in God the Father than in christology. Protestant modernists balked at almost every article of the creed until some managed to resuscitate it in the role of poetry.

By the last half of the century the appeal to historical revelation as the source of knowledge of God ran into contrary headwinds. History's demonstrative value was increasingly questioned as more and more scholars recognized that historical methodology cannot prove transcendence, that historical events are not scientifically verifiable by duplication, that the historian's presuppositions condition his interpretation, and that his explanations cannot lay claim to scientific objectivity. As Milet notes: "This change of opinion about the value of historical methodology had the gravest consequences for the generation... between 1950 and 1970; reference to the 'God of Jesus Christ' was in turn undermined. Here theocentricity lost its last foundation" (1981:144). The inability of history to establish itself as normative is now an accepted theme; the danger today is ahistoricism. For Michel Foucault each movement of thought has its particular meaning within its own epoch, and not even the whole transcends human consciousness. To seek a universal message from Judeo-Christian history or from any other is therefore considered pointless.

Resistance to a heightened christocentricity thereafter becomes destructive of both christology and theology. Since philosophical reasoning could not conclusively establish faith in God and since historical method could not conclusively justify faith in Christ, the novel possibility loomed for some commentators to resist modern atheism by viewing Christ as a superman, a towering human personality worthy of our trust. The human lordship of Jesus calling for personal adherence to him as an historical figure—quite apart from any explicit exposition of transcendence—gains prominence. This tendency to ignore transcendence Milet finds in the Protestant theologian Dietrich Bonhoeffer and in Catholic scholars like Hans Kung and P. Schoonenberg. Rudolf Bultmann wholly negates ontological transcendence and demythologizes Jesus Christ.

Milet charts the subsequent rise of "atheistic Christianity" after the 1960s in two developments. "First of all, Christ is 'isolated' completely from all reference to a God, then, ... after the acceptance of the idea of 'the death of God,' we are presented with a 'powerful and solitary' Christ who challenges humanity single-handed and saves it from misery by the sole virtue of his human qualities" (1981:190).

The Protestant theologians Kierkegaard and Barth (Milet would also add Luther) contribute to this theme of Christ's "solitude." For all Barth's use of dialectic, however, his express intentions were theocentric. But Bonhoeffer moves more pointedly toward "Christianity without God," i.e., christology without a transcendent deity.

Since contemporary philosophy rejects divine transcendence—
and the masses get along quite comfortably without God—a
growing number of Protestant and Catholic theologians also
proceed to elaborate Christianity without transcendence. This
is especially the case with American death of God writers
who "'de-deified' Christ." Tillich derailed God for Being itself, and for truth looked to Christ the man. On the European scene Bultmann forged his christology in the context of
Heidegger's rejection of transcendence.

For Schoonenberg, Christ stimulates mankind's dreams of
God as super-model of a humanity intrinsically immanent
in the human species. Milet cites similarly-minded theologians from France, Spain, Germany, Holland, Belgium, and
Switzerland. He notes as an extreme outcome of English
Anglican bishop John A. T. Robinson's speculations in *Honest
to God* the readiness of some writers even to insist that
radical atheism is the necessary presupposition of faith in
Christ. Among American contributors to the death of God
theme were Paul Van Buren (1963), and Harvey Cox (1965),
and in a somewhat different way, Gabriel N. Vahanian (1961).

Radical Protestant theology which, especially after 1970,
gained influence among Catholic theologians, was deliberately devoted to an atheistic Christianity, particularly in a
dialectical context. In Catholic circles, however, a practical
rather than theoretical form of atheistic Christianity emerged
to greater prominence in the theology of revolution and in
subsequent liberation theology, which theologians projected
as a reevaluation of both Marxist and Christian doctrines.
Joseph Comblin (1970) depicts Christ as a revolutionary. J.
Girardi uses Marxist social analysis and then boldly pursues
a classless society as a Christian rather than Marxist program. Others impoverished Christianity to a form of humanism based loosely on values that Jesus supported—brotherhood,
compassion, justice, integrity. Here "the last vestiges of theocentric faith are renounced," comments Milet; "there is no
longer talk of sin or of the necessity of salvation or of
penance or even of the beyond; the themes of grace and
providence are abandoned. Only 'social' themes are taken
into consideration. A Christian is someone who engages in
social struggle" (1981:203). No need remains for prayer and

contemplation. "If things continue to evolve in accordance with this logic, after fifty or a hundred years, Christianity will end up by being reduced to a humanitarian movement" (ibid., 204).

Catholic moral theology turned at mid-century, Milet notices, from the natural morality of Thomas Aquinas, which is basically theocentric in context, to a new and deliberately christocentric form in which Christ became the ultimate norm. Definitive for ethics is the Christ of the Gospels and no longer the cardinal virtues supplemented by the theological virtues. Milet protests the subsequent rise of a non-directive morality, one that sets aside objective principles, and appeals only to 'the spirit of Jesus,' and seeks from this to infer what Jesus would do or would have done in our circumstances. In the 1960s social action predicated on an appeal to Jesus emerges in a quite unexpected way as a program of revolutionary involvement and takes the form of radical christocentricity in which reference to a transcendent God virtually vanishes.

Milet's deepest concern is that Catholic theology began to welcome christocentricity exclusive of theocentricity: outside of knowledge of Christ there is no knowledge of God. Pierre Teilhard de Chardin championed cosmochristocentricity—the entire history of the cosmos finds its Omega-point in the mystical person of Christ.

Modern science at mid-century provided a new opening for theocentricity, Milet avers. It had rejected nineteenth century determinism and left the door ajar, alongside a more modest view of law as approximate postulation, and without methodological conflict, for metaphysical inquiry based on other approaches. Prominent nuclear physicists led by researchers at Princeton began speaking again of a preexisting divine Logos reflected in the cosmos's intelligibility to mankind (cf. R. Ryer, 1977). Their decoding of the universe seemed to presuppose a superior rationality, a Logos who orders the cosmos, a theocentricity which in the absence of a revelational axiom readily accommodated pantheistic overtones.

Yet, precisely at this time, avant-garde theologians pursued an exclusive christocentricity, and rejected any possibility of reconciliation with science. They called for sheer religious faith—for "irrational adherence to Christ as a religious guide"—as Milet summarizes their trend toward pure fideism (1981:167-68). Alongside this development emerged both a social and political christocentricity—the former often assuming compatibility with the spirit of Jesus and affirming that society is moving inevitably toward socialism, and the latter foregoing any universal principles of political order but focusing instead on sayings of Jesus and moving toward "a kind of 'christocracy'" (1981:172). In short, Milet deprecates "hyperchristocentric purists" (ibid. 173) who dream of a pure Christianity in present-day history, while he also deplores radical christocentricity which periodically disdains any and all theocentricity.

Since 1970, Milet observes, a reaction has nonetheless emerged in the direction of theocentricity (ibid.,173-74) and has even led at times to "a bogus christocentricity, a vague humanism" (ibid., 178). Shaped by this tendency "an evolution has continued" in popular worship "from the first variations on Berulle's christocentricity to the last variations of the pagan christocentricity of pop music and the image of Jesus Christ Superstar" (ibid., 182). Milet assesses Vatican II as more theocentric than Vatican I, yet despite striving for balance nonetheless accommodating christocentrism more than was traditionally acceptable, and at times reflecting a bias towards it.

Milet has the impression that "during the period 1960-1970, and particularly after the Council...two churches are being called on to live in the bosom of one community traditionally called Catholicism: a church living in obedience to God and his commandments and a church which lives in accord with the appeals of Christ and his invitation to the love of men" (1981:189). Milet emphasizes that the avant-garde theologians scarcely speak for Catholicism as a whole, even as, we may add, Protestant ecumenical frontiersmen usually fail to reflect a vast evangelical orthodox constituency. North American and African Catholicism largely escaped christocentrism because of its resistance to dialectical thought and its firm sense of the reality of nature and of God. The reinforcement of theocentrism comes from works that criticize the immanentistic theologies of Bonhoeffer, Tillich, Kung, and others

and who, stressing the transcendent character of the content
of faith, correlate divine revelation and the 'metahistorical'
character of the mission of Christ.

Yet much recent French religious literature focuses on God
in terms of speculative metaphysics and virtually ignores
Jesus Christ. The reaction against christocentrism thus takes
the form of secular philosophy of religion by reviving un-
promising Thomistic theory, whereas current philosophy of
science now is prone—as was Augustine—to begin with faith
in search of understanding.

It is possible, indeed, to view the tension between theocentricity and christocentricity since the mid-twentieth century somewhat differently than does Milet. Milet's comments
are not uninfluenced by the official Catholic view that human reason unaided by revelation can logically prove God's
existence simply on the basis of inference from empirical
observation. The Thomistic contrast of philosophy and theology is evident in Milet's comment that the theologian and
the philosopher are not on the same wave length, theology
being based on revelation and faith, and philosophy "only on
reason," so that contact between them is impossible (ibid.,
249, n.6). One can contend, by contrast, that Christ is the
mediator of all supernatural revelation and hence of all
knowledge of God whether by general revelation given in the
cosmos and history and in man as bearer of the *imago dei,* or
by special revelation, both scriptural and incarnational. Thus
to say there is no knowledge of God except through Christ
need not restrict such knowledge to Jesus of Nazareth.

Augustine, Anselm, and the Reformers rejected the notion
that philosophy is a genre wholly distinct from theology, and
they did not view Christian philosophy as necessarily hostile
to theocentrism. If all truth is God's truth, and the Logos of
God became incarnate in Jesus of Nazareth, and if the
eternal Logos (preexistent, incarnate and now glorified) is
the mediator of all divine revelation (cf. Henry, 1974-8:2:11-12;
3:164-66), no basis remains for making metaphysics an au-
tonomous science.

That is not to say—except in a qualified way—that there
can be no thought of God without thought of Christ. To be
sure, the Scottish professor of apologetics James Orr argued

persuasively in his *The Christian View of God and the World* (1889) that the incarnation can with some legitimacy be regarded as the *raison d'etre* of creation. "By its central place in the Christian system," Orr states, the truth of the Incarnation illuminates and transforms everyother doctrine (ibid., 33). That Christ orders and conditions all else, and is central in the history of creation and redemption, and that the universe subsists in Him, need not be incompatible with the emphasis that as the divine executive in creation and salvation He is the Logos through whom the triune God expresses His will. With the weakening of natural theology and natural law schemes the case for a divine-command morality has gained ground over against natural morality, alongside the linkage of moral claims to the incarnate and risen Christ. The fact that objective moral principles are as old as the history of man—in fact, much older—does not mean that morality must be detached from Christ as the divine agent in creation and the *imago Dei* that man bears in a more limited and now sullied way.

The christocentric tendency, unfortunately, came to involve not a comprehensive Logos-doctrine, but a rejection of the serviceability of philosophical analysis, logical tests, and cognitive systematization. Here the teaching of Christ is disjoined from all other theoretical considerations. A separation of christocentrism from theocentricism, or of theocentricism from christocentrism, leads in the end to a revival of deism which cannot do justice to either prong of the discussion. Evangelical Protestants have no more obligation than orthodox Catholics to consider salvation only in Jesus Christ as exclusive of the ontological reality of a transcendent God. Milet has put the matter well: "The Christian must put his or her faith, with equal fervour, both in a God who transcends the world..., and in a Christ, the terrestrial incarnation of this God and savior of men" (1981:215).

Secular liberal arts learning today is cognitively more prone to naturalism than to theism, whether speculative or christological. Milet is disturbed, as indeed he should be, by the recent theological loss of the transcendent. Many modern history books disregard Jesus Christ and treat him as a nonentity, a stance that Voltaire encouraged by giving Jesus only a single passing mention in his account of history. To deliberately exclude Jesus from supposedly informed academic studies takes a herculean amount of disinterest or of religious illiteracy. A Christianity without Christ would revert to Judaism or drift toward Islam; it would lose distinctive identity among the world religions. If one empties Christianity into the 'death of God' or into liberation theology, then, as Milet indicates, it fades from the great living religions into a universal humanism. Its authentic survival requires a repudiation of such monstrosities as radical christocentricity and of either deistic or immanentistic theocentricity. Yet Jesus stands apart from the crowd from the moment of his entry into this world by the virgin-birth to the day of his exit from it by bodily resurrection. For almost everybody he remains in some way singularly unique—if not as the sure way to God, then in other and lesser acknowledgments. Many who are reluctant to view him as "man for God" are constrained at least to view him as "man for man." Those who hold that he exemplifies God's love for man usually mean more than that he is one of a class and find his life indicative of the essence of *agape*.

Milet identifies Catholicism as essentially a bipolar religion, and thus seems to obscure the orthodox credal insistence on Jesus' consubstantiality both with the Father and with humanity. Yet orthodox Catholic theologians like Joseph Siri (1981), are rightly concerned lest the pressure of modern philosophical movements will lead current christological study to dilute scriptural representations of Christ. Siri objects, as does Milet, to a Christology "from below." Milet's sociological analysis of trends suggests at times that proper insistence on the full humanity of Jesus requires a break with his divine transcendence, to the detriment of the Christian affirmation of consubstantiality. Some critics of Milet even profess to find a new Arian mood in his approach, at the expense of theocentricism [cf. Thomas Molnar, (1987:189)].

Milet anticipates the emergence of a new scholasticism—a new era of theology—rising from quantum physics. His projections run counter to the expectations of philosophical deconstructionists. But his postulation as a starting point of an ontology establishing "a network of noetic structures" that "escape Kantian criticism and even Husserlian criticism" (1981:227) is sound. If one begins with the transcendent living God in his self-revelation, the sovereign triune God incarnate in Jesus Christ, and tests its derivatives for logical consistency, and invokes Scripture as a verifying principle, "a period of great metaphysical vigor" could indeed reappear, albeit in the tradition of Augustine and Anselm and the Reformers. A carefully nuanced theocentricity and christocentricity could then emerge in equilibrium, each strengthening the other, rather than veering either toward exclusive theocentricity or toward exclusive christocentricity. A sound theology of the incarnation must be shaped in the context of theocentricity as its starting point, and theocentricity must itself be formulated in trinitarian and incarnational terms if it is truly Christian. The implications for life no less than for doctrine must be lucidly in view, so that in adoration of the Godhead the believer will worship the Father through the Son to whom "every knee shall bow" (Phil 2:10), and anticipate the day when the Son "delivers the kingdom to God the Father" (1 Cor 15:24).

Bibliography

Ahlstrom, Sydney E. and Jonathan S. Carey.

1985   *An American Reformation: A Documentary History of Unitarian Christianity*. Middletown, Conn.: Wesleyan University Press.

Augustine.

1960   *The Confessions of St. Augustine*. Trans. John K. Ryan. Garden City, NY: Doubleday.

Baillie, D. M.

1948   *God Was in Christ: An Essay on Incarnation and Atonement*. London: Farber & Farber.

Balchin, John F.

1982   "Paul, Wisdom, and Christ" in *Christ the Lord*, 204-19. Ed. Harold H. Rowden. Leicester: Inter-Varsity.

Barth, Karl.

1936-61 *Church Dogmatics*. Trans. G. W. Bromiley and T. F. Torrance. 4 vols. Edinburgh: T & T Clark.

1949   *Dogmatics in Outline*. New York: Philosophical Library.

Bayer, Hans F.

1986   *Jesus' Predictions of Vindication and Resurrection: The Provenance, Meaning and Correlation of the Synoptic Predictions*. Tubingen: Mohr-Siebeck.

Berkhof, Hendrikus.

1979   *Christian Faith: An Introduction to the Study of the Faith*. Grand Rapids: Eerdmans.

Berkley, Robert F.

1982   "Christological Perspectives: The Context of Current Dis-
        cussions," in *Christological Perspectives: Essays in Honor
        of Harvey K. McArthur.* Ed. Robert F. Berkley and Sarah
        A. Edwards. New York: Pilgrim.

Blaising, Craig A.

1981   "Chalcedon and Christology." *Bibliotheca Sacra* 138: 326-37.

Blocher, Henri.

1987   *Christologie.* Vaux-sur-Seine: Faculte de Theologie Evan-
        geleque.

Boers, H.

1970   "Jesus and the Christian Faith: New Testament Chris-
        tology since Bousset's *Kyrios Christos,*" *Journal of Biblical
        Literature* 89: 450-56.

Borg, Marcus J.

1987   *Jesus: A New Vision.* San Francisco: Harper & Row.

1988   "A Renaissance in Jesus Studies," *Theology Today* 45:
        280-92.

Boslooper, Thomas.

1962   *The Virgin Birth.* Philadelphia: Westminster.

Bousset, Wilhelm.

1970   *Kyrios Christos.* Gottingen: Vandenhoeck & Ruprecht, 1913,
        1921. Trans. John B. Steeley from the 5th German ed. of
        1964. Nashville and New York: Abingdon.

Bowden, John.

1988   *Jesus: The Unanswered Questions.* Nashville: Abingdon.

Braun, H.

1957   "Der Sinn der neutestamentlich Christologie." *Zeitschrift
        fur Theologie und Kirche* 54: 41-77.

Brown, Colin.

1985   *That You May Believe: Miracles and Faith Then and Now.*
        Grand Rapids: Eerdmans.

Brown, Harold O. J.

1984   *Heresies: The Image of Christ in the Mirror of Heresy and
        Orthodoxy from the Apostles to the Present.* Garden City,
        N.Y.: Doubleday.

Brown, Herbert.

1979   *Jesus of Nazareth: The Man and His Time.* Philadelphia:
        Fortress.

Brown, Raymond E.

1966-70 *The Gospel According to John.* 2 vols. *The Anchor Bible.*
        Garden City, NY: Doubleday.

1967   *Jesus, God and Man.* New York: Macmillan.

Bruce, F. F.

1982   "The Background to the Son of Man Sayings," in *Christ
        the Lord*, 50-70. Ed. Harold H. Rowden. Leicester: Inter-
        Varsity.

1978   Essay in *Jesus: God, Ghost or Guru?* Ed. Jon A. Buell and
        O. Quentin Hyder. Grand Rapids: Zondervan.

Brunner, Emil.

1950   *The Christian Doctrine of God.* Philadelphia: Westmin-
        ster.

Bultmann, Rudolf.

1955   *Essays: Philosophical and Theological.* London: SCM.

1958   *Jesus Christ and Mythology.* New York: Scribner's.

1984   *New Testament and Mythology.* Trans. Schubert M. Ogden.
        Philadelphia: Fortress.

Butler, Christopher.

1977   "Jesus and Later Orthodoxy" in *The Truth of God Incar-
        nate.* Ed. Michael Green. Grand Rapids: Eerdmans.

Caird, G. B.

1968   "The Development of the Doctrine of Christ in the New
        Testament," in *Christ for Us Today*. Ed. Norman Pittenger.
        London: SCM.

Caird, John.

1895-96 *The Fundamental Ideas of Christianity*. Gifford Lectures.
        Glasgow: J. MacLehose. 1899.

Carey, George.

1978   *God Incarnate: Meeting the Contemporary Challenges to a
        Classic Christian Doctrine*. Downers Grove, Ill.: InterVarsity.

Carnley, Peter.

1987   *The Structure of Resurrection Belief*. Oxford: Clarendon.

Carson, D. A.

1982   "Christological Ambiguities in Matthew" in *Christ the
        Lord*, 97-114. Ed. H. H. Rowden. Leicester: Inter-Varsity.

Charlesworth, James H.

1988   *Jesus Within Judaism: New Light from Exciting Archaeo-
        logical Discoveries*. New York: Doubleday.

Clark, Gordon H.

1979   *Colossians, Another Commentary on an Inexhaustible Mes-
        sage*. Phillipsburg, N.J.: Presbyterian and Reformed.

1988   *The Incarnation*. Jefferson, Ind.: The Trinity Foundation.

Clebsch, William.

1979   *Christianity in European History*. New York: Oxford Uni-
        versity Press.

Cobb, John B.

1969   "Wolfhart Pannenberg's Jesus—God and Man." *JR* 49:

1975   *Christ in a Pluralistic Age*. Philadelphia: Westminster.

Comblin, Joseph.
1970   *Theologie de la Revolution, Theorie.* Paris: Editions Luniversitaires.

Cook, Bernard.
1990   Review of *The Word of Life,* by Thomas C. Oden. *Theology Today* 47: 216.

Cotterell, F. P.
1982   "The Christology of Islam," in *Christ the Lord,* 282-89. Ed. H. H. Rowden. Leicester: Inter-Varsity.

Countryman, L. William.
1982   "Review of *Christology in the Making." Church History* 51: 335.

Cox, Harvey.
1965   *The Secular City.* New York: Macmillan.

Craig, William.
1987   Review of *The Logic of God Incarnate,* by Thomas V. Morris. *Journal of the Evangelical Theological Society* 30:493-94.

Crawford, Robert.
1985   *The Saga of God Incarnate.* Pretoria: University of South Africa Press.

Creed, John Martin.
1930   "Recent Tendencies in English Christology" in *Mysterium Christi.* Ed. G. K. A. Bell and D. Adolf Deismann. London: Longmans, Green.

Crites, S.
1981   "Unfinished Figure: On Theology and the Imagination" in *Unfinished . . . : Essays in Honor of Ray Hart,* 155-84. *Journal of the American Academy of Religion* Thematic Studies 4811. Ed. Mark L. Taylor. Chicago: Scholars.

Cullmann, Oscar.
1963   *The Christology of the New Testament.* Trans. Shirley C. Guthrie and Hans A. M. Hall. Philadelphia: Westminster.

Cupitt, Don.
1977   "The Christ of Christendom," in *The Myth of God Incarnate,* 133-47, Ed. John Hick. Philadelphia: Westminster.
1979   *The Debate About Christ.* London: SCM.

Davis, Charles.
1976   "Religion and the Sense of the Sacred." *Proceedings of the Catholic Theological Society of America.*

Davis, Stephen T., ed.
1988   "Jesus Christ: Savior or Guru?" in *Encountering Jesus: A Debate on Christology.* Atlanta: John Knox.

Davies, W. D.
1948, 1967 *Paul and Rabbinic Judaism.* New York: Harper.

De Chardin, T.
1960   *The Divine Milieu.* New York: Harper & Row.
1961   *Hymn of the Universe.* New York: Harper & Row.

De Lacy, D. R.
1982   "'One Lord' in Pauline Christology" in *Christ the Lord,* 191-203. Ed. H. H. Rowden. Leicester: Inter-Varsity.

Dulles, Avery.
1985   *Models of Revelation.* Garden City, N.Y.: Doubleday.

Dunn, J. D. G.
1977   *Unity and Diversity in the New Testament: An Inquiry into the Character of Earliest Christianity.* London: SCM.
1980   *Christology in the Making: An Inquiry into the Origins of the Doctrine of the Incarnation.* London: SCM.

Easton, Burton Scott.
1928   *The Gospel Before the Gospels.* New York: Scribner's.

Eckstein, Yachiel.
1984   *What Christians Should Know about Jews and Judaism.* Waco: Word.

Ellul, Jacques.
1983   *Living Faith.* San Francisco: Harper & Row.

Elwell, Walter A., ed.
1988   *The Baker Encyclopedia of the Bible.* Grand Rapids: Baker.

Erickson, Millard J.
1991   *The Word Became Flesh.* Grand Rapids: Baker.

Fergusen, John.
1980   *Jesus in the Tide of Time: An Historical Study.* London: Routledge & Kegan Paul.

France, R. T.
1982   "The Worship of Jesus: A Neglected Factor in Christological Debate?" in *Christ the Lord,* 17-36. Ed. H. H. Rowden. Leicester: Inter-Varsity.
1986   *The Evidence for Jesus.* Downers Grove, Ill.: InterVarsity.

Fredricksen, Paula.
1988   *From Jesus to Christ: The Origin of New Testament Images of Jesus.* New Haven: Yale University Press.

Frend, W. H. C.
1972   *The Rise of Monophysite Movement: Chapters in the History of the Church in the Fifth and Sixth Centuries.* New York: Cambridge University Press.
1984   *The Rise of Christianity.* Philadelphia: Fortress.

Fuller, Reginald H.
1965   *The Foundations of New Testament Christology.* London: Lutterworth.

Galtier, Paul.

1939 *L'Unite du Christ, Etre...Personne...Conscience.* Paris: G. Beauchesne.

Goppelt, L.

1981 *Theology of the New Testament.* Trans. John E. Alsop. Ed. Jürgen Roloff and G. Rap. Grand Rapids: Eerdmans.

Gordon, Cyrus H.

1983 "Jewish Reactions to Christian Borrowings" in *The Word of the Lord Shall Go Forth.* Ed. Carol L. Meyers and M. O'Conner. Winina Lake, Ind.: Eisenbrauns.

Gore, Charles.

1922 *Belief in Christ.* New York: Scribner's.

Gray, P. T. R.

1979 *The Defense of Chalcedon in the East.* Leiden: Brill.

Grillmeier, Aloys.

1965 *Christ in Christian Tradition 1: From the Apostolic Age to Chalcedon.* Atlanta: John Knox, 1957. Rev. ed.

1975 "'Piscatorrie'—Aristolice. Zur Bedeutung der 'Formel' in den seit Chalkedan getrennten Kirchen" in *Christologische Forschungen und Perspektiven.* Freiburg.

Groothuis, Douglas.

1990 *Revealing the New Age Jesus.* Downers Grove, Ill.: InterVarsity.

Guinness, Os.

1973 *The Dust of Death.* Downers Grove, Ill.: InterVarsity.

Gundry, Robert.

1981 *New Testament Theology.* Downers Grove, Ill.: InterVarsity.

Gunton, Colin.

1983 *Yesterday and Today: A Study in Continuities in Christology.* Grand Rapids: Eerdmans.

1990 "Using and Being Used: Scripture and Systematic Theology." *Theology Today* 47:248-59.

Guthrie, D.
1975 "Jesus Christ" in *The Zondervan Pictorial Encyclopedia of the Bible*. Vol. 3. Ed. M. C. Tenney. Grand Rapids: Zondervan.
1981 *New Testament Theology*. Downers Grove, Ill.: InterVarsity.

Gutierez, Gustavo.
1973 *A Theology of Liberation*. Trans. Caridad Inda, Sr. and John Eagleson. Maryknoll, N.Y.: Orbis.

Hagner, Donald A.
1984 *The Jewish Reclamation of Jesus*. Grand Rapids: Zondervan.

Hahn, Ferdinand.
1969 *The Titles of Jesus in Christology: Their History in Early Christianity*. Trans. H. Knight and G. Ogg. London: Lutterworth.

Haire, J. L. M.
1956 "On Behalf of Chalcedon" in *Essays in Christology for Karl Barth*. Ed. T. H. L. Parker. London: Lutterworth.

Harnack, Adolf von.
1961 *History of Dogma*. 7 vols. in 4. Reprint. New York: Dover.

Harris, M. J.
1980 "Titus 2:13 and the Deity of Christ" in *Pauline Studies*. Ed. D. A. Hagner and M. J. Harris. Grand Rapids: Eerdmans.

Hauerwas, Stanley.
1989 *Resident Aliens: Life in the Christian Colony*. Nashville: Abingdon.

Hemer, Colin.
1989 *The Book of Acts in the Setting of Hellenistic History*. Tubingen: J. C. B. Mohr.

Hengel, Martin.
1976   *The Son of God: The Origin of Christology and the History of Jewish-Hellenistic Religion*. Trans. John Bowden. Philadelphia: Fortress.

Henry, Carl F. H.
1979   *God, Revelation, and Authority*. 6 vols. Waco: Word.

Hick, John.
1973   "Towards a Christian Theology of Other Religions." *God and the Universe of Faiths*. London: Macmillan.
1977   *The Myth of God Incarnate*. Philadelphia: Westminster.
1980   *God Has Many Names*. Philadelphia: Westminster.

Higgins, A. J. B.
1981   *The Son of Man in the Teachings of Jesus*. Cambridge: Cambridge University Press.

Hodge, A. A.
1860   *Outlines of Theology*. New York: Carter & Brothers.

Hodge, Charles.
1872-73 *Systematic Theology*. New York: Scribner's.

Hodgson, Leonard.
1968   *For Faith and Freedom*. Gifford Lectures (1955-57). London: SCM.
1928   *And Was Made Man*. London: Longmans, Green.

Hodgson, Peter.
1971   *Jesus—Word and Presence*. Philadelphia: Fortress.

Houlden, J. L.
1975   "The Place of the New Testament" in *What About the New Testament?: Essays in Honor of Christopher Evans*. Ed. M. Hooker and C. Hickling. London: SCM.

Hoskyns, Sir Edwyn and Noel Davey.
1931   *The Riddle of the New Testament*. London: Farber & Farber.

Houston, James M.
1980   *I Believe in the Creator*. Grand Rapids: Eerdmans.

Jenson, Robert W.
1982   *The Triune Identity. God According to the Gospel*. Philadelphia: Fortress.
1984   *Christian Dogmatics*. Ed. Robert W. Jensen and Carl E. Braaten. Philadelphia: Fortress.

Jeremias, Joachim.
1965   *The Central Message of the New Testament*. Philadelphia: Fortress.

Jewett, Paul K.
1975   "Monotheism" in *The Zondervan Pictorial Encyclopedia of the Bible*. Ed. Merrill C. Tenney, 4:271-72. Grand Rapids: Zondervan.

Kim, Seyoon.
1981   *The Origin of Paul's Gospel*. Tubingen: Mohr.

Knitter, Paul.
1979   "Jesus-Buddha-Krishna: Still Present?," *Journal of Ecumenical Studies* 16: 651-71.

Kung, Hans.
1976   *On Being Christian*. Garden City, N.Y.: Doubleday.

Kraus, C. Norman.
1987   *Jesus Christ Our Lord*. Scottsdale, Penn.: Herald.

Lane, A. N. S.
1982   "Christology Beyond Chalcedon" in *Christ the Lord*, 257-81. Ed. H. H. Rowden. Leicester: Inter-Varsity.

Lapide, Pinchas and Jurgen Moltmann.
1981   *Jewish Monotheism and Christian Trinitarian Doctrine: A Dialogue.* Philadelphia: Fortress.

Lapide, Pinchas.
1984   *The Resurrection of Jesus: A Jewish Perspective.* Minneapolis: Augsburg.

Lawton, J. S.
1943   *Conflict in Christology: A Study of British and American Christology from 1889-1914.* New York: Macmillan.

Laymon, Charles M., ed.
1971   *Interpreter's One-Volume Commentary on the Bible.* Nashville: Abingdon.

Leivestad, Ragnar.
1987   *Jesus in His Own Perspective: An Examination of his Sayings, Actions, and Eschatological Titles.* Trans. David E. Aune. Minneapolis: Augsburg.

Lewis, C. S.
1970   *God in the Dock: Essays on Theology and Ethics.* Ed. Walter Hooper. Grand Rapids: Eerdmans.

Lindars, Barnabas.
1983   *Jesus Son of Man: A Fresh Examination of the Son of Man Sayings in the Gospels.* Grand Rapids: Eerdmans.

Long, William R.
1989   "Martin Hengel on Early Christianity." *Religious Studies Review* 15:3.

Lustiger, Jean-Marie Cardinal.
1986   *Dare to Believe: Addresses, Sermons, Interviews, 1981-1984.* New York: Crossroad.

Mack, Burton L.
1988   *A Myth of Innocence: Mark and Christian Origins.* Philadelphia: Fortress.

McDonald, H. Dermont.

1968 *Jesus—Human and Divine*. London: Pickering & Inglis.

1975 "Christ's Two Natures: The Significance of Chalcedon Today." *Christianity Today* 19 (26 Sept.): 12-14.

McGrath, Allister E.

1986 *The Making of Modern German Christology*. Cambridge: Basil Blackwell.

Mackintosh, H. R.

1913 *The Doctrine of the Person of Christ*. Edinburgh: T. & T. Clark. Reprint. New York: Charles Scribner's, 1942.

Manson, William.

1943 *Jesus the Messiah*. London: Hodder & Stoughton.

Mascall, E. L.

1943 *He Who Is*. New York: Longmans, Green.

Marshall, I. Howard.

1976 *The Origins of New Testament Christology*. Downers Grove, Ill.: InterVarsity.

Marxen, W.

1968 "The Resurrection of Jesus as a Historical and Theological Problem" in *The Significance of the Message of the Resurrection for Faith in Jesus Christ*. Ed. C. F. D. Moule. Naperville, Ill.: Alec R. Allenson.

Metzger, Bruce M.

1973 "The Punctuation of Rom. 9:5" in *Christ and Spirit in the New Testament*. Ed. Barnabas Lindars and Stephen S. Smalley. Cambridge: University Press.

Meyendorff, J.

1975 *Christ in Eastern European Thought*. Washington, D.C.: Corpus.

1979 *Byzantine Theology: Historical Trends*. Washington, D.C.: Corpus.

Micklem, N.

1930   "A Modern Approach to Christology" in *Mysterium Christi.* Ed. G. K. A. Bell and D. Adolf Deismann. London: Longmans, Green.

Milet, Jean.

1981   *God or Christ.* Trans. J. Bowden. London: SCM.

Molnar, Thomas.

1987   *The Pagan Temptation.* Grand Rapids: Eerdmans.

Moltmann, Jurgen.

1967   *Theology of Hope.* New York: Harper & Row.

1981   *The Trinity and the Kingdom: The Doctrine of God.* New York: Harper & Row.

Montefiore, C. G.

1972   *The Old Testament and After.* 1923. Reprint. New York: Arno.

Morris, Leon.

1987   *Jesus is the Christ: Essays in the Theology of John.* Grand Rapids: Eerdmans.

Morris, Richard.

1983   *Evolution and Human Nature.* New York: Seaview/ Putnam.

Morris, Thomas V.

1986   *The Logic of God Incarnate.* Ithica, NY: Cornell University Press.

1988   "Understanding God Incarnate." *Asbury Theological Journal* 43: 63-77.

1989   "The Metaphysics of God Incarnate," in *Incarnation, Trinity and Atonement.* Ed. Ronald Feinstra and Cornelius Plantinga. Notre Dame: University of Notre Dame Press.

Moule, C. F. D.

1962   *The Birth of the New Testament.* Harper's New Testament Commentaries. New York: Harper & Row.

1977   *The Origin of Christology.* Cambridge: University Press.

Muller, Richard A.

1986   "Directions in the Study of Barth's Christology." *Westminster Theological Journal* 48: 119-34.

Mussner, Frank.

1981   Essay in *Judische Existenz und die Erneuerung der christlichen Theologie.* Munich: Christian Kaiser.

Nash, Ronald.

1984   *Christian Faith and Historical Understanding.* Grand Rapids: Zondervan.

Nietzsche, Friedrich Wilhelm.

1972   *The Antichrist.* 1930. Reprint. New York: Arno.

Nock, A. D.

1972   *Essays on Religion and the Ancient World.* Cambridge: Harvard University Press.

Norris, Richard A., ed. and trans.

1980   *The Christological Controversy.* Philadelphia: Fortress.

Novak, David.

1991   "A Jewish Theological Understanding of Christianity in Our Time." *First Things* 9 (January): 26-33.

Novak, Michael.

1983   *Confessions of a Catholic.* San Francisco: Harper & Row.

O'Collins, G. G.

1968   "The Theology of Revelation in Some Recent Discussion." Ph.D. dissertation, Cambridge University.

1987   "Jesus," in *The Encyclopedia of Religion.* Ed. Mircea Eliade, 8:15-28. New York: Macmillan.

Oden, Thomas.

1989   *The Word of Life, Systematic Theology.* San Francisco: Harper & Row.

Orr, James.

1893   *The Christian View of God and the World.* Edinburgh: A. Elliot.

Osborn, Robert T.

1985   "The Christian Blasphemy." *Journal of the American Academy of Religion* 53:3: 339-63.

O'Shaughnessy, Thomas.

1948   *The Koranic Concept of the Word of God.* Rome: Pontificio Instituto Biblico.

Pannenberg, W.

1970   "Nachwert" in *Geschichte, Offenbarung, Glaube.* Ed. Ignace Berten. Munich: Claudias.

1977   *Jesus—God and Man.* Trans. Lewis L. Wilkins and Duane A. Priebe. 2d ed. Philadelphia: Westminster.

Parrinder, Geoffrey.

1977   *Jesus in the Qur'an.* Oxford: University Press.

Payne, Phillip B.

1981   "The Authenticity of the Parables of Jesus" in *Gospel Perspectives 2.* Ed. R. T. France and David Wenham. Sheffield: JSOT Press.

Pelikan, Jaroslav.

1986   *Jesus Through the Centuries: His Place in the History of Culture.* New Haven: Yale University Press.

Pittenger, Norman.

1970   *Christology Reconsidered.* London: SCM.

Pregeant, Russell.

1978   *Christology Beyond Dogma: Matthew's Christ in Process Hermeneutic.* Missoula: Scholars.

Pinnock, Clark.
1982   "The Many Christs of Current Theology," *Christianity Today* 26:6 (19 March).

Preus, Robert.
1986   "The Living God," in Summit III Papers of the International Council on Biblical Inerrancy. Ed. Kenneth Kantzer. Walnut Creek, Calif.: International Council on Biblical Inerrancy.

Rahner, Karl.
1974   *Sacramentum Mundi*
        Theological Investigations, 1: God, Christ, Mary, Grace. Trans. Cornelius Ernst. New York: Seabury.

Ramm, Bernard.
1985   *An Evangelical Christology—Ecumenic and Historic.* Nashville: Thomas Nelson.

Reuther, Rosemary.
1974   *Faith and Fratricide.* New York: Seabury.

Richard, Earl.
1988   *Jesus: One and Many: The Christological Concept of the New Testament Authors.* Wilmington, Del.: Michael Glazier.

Richardson, Alan and John S. Bowden, eds.
1983   *The Westminster Dictionary of Theology.* Philadelphia: Westminster.

Richardson, Cyril C.
1958   *The Doctrine of the Trinity.* Nashville: Abingdon.

Robinson, David.
1985   *The Unitarians and the Universalists.* Westport, Conn.: Greenwood.

Robinson, John A. T.
1973   *The Human Face of God.* Philadelphia: Westminster.

Roth, Cecil and Geoffrey Wigoder, eds.
1975 *The New Standard Jewish Encyclopedia*. London: W. H. Allen.

Rowden, Harold H., ed.
1982 *Christ the Lord*. Leicester: Inter-Varsity.

Runia, Klaas.
1982 "Karl Barth's Christology" in *Christ the Lord*, 299-310. Ed. Harold H. Rowden. Leicester: Inter-Varsity.
1984 *The Present-Day Christological Debate*. Downers Grove, Ill.: InterVarsity.

Ryer, Raymond.
1977 *La Gnose de Princeton*. Paris: Le Livre de Poche.

Sanders, E. P.
1987 *Jesus and the Spiral of Violence*. San Francisco: Harper & Row.

Schabert, Jane.
1987 *The Illegitimacy of Jesus*. San Francisco: Harper & Row.

Schillebeeckx, Edward.
1979 *Jesus: An Experiment in Christology*. New York: Seabury.

Schlossberg, Herbert.
1983 *Idols for Destruction*. Nashville: Thomas Nelson.

Schoeps, H. J.
1961 *Paul: The Theology of the Apostle in the Light of Jewish History*. Philadelphia: Westminster.

Schoonenberg, Piet.
1971 *The Christ*. Trans. Della Conling. New York: Herder & Herder.

Schweitzer, Albert.

1954   *The Quest of the Historical Jesus*. 1910. Reprint. New York: Black.

Shedd, W. G. T.

1971   *Dogmatic Theology*. 1888. Reprint. Grand Rapids: Zondervan.

Sheehan, Thomas.

1986   *The First Coming: How the Kingdom of God Became Christianity*. New York: Random.

Sherwin-White, A. N.

1963   *Roman Society and Roman Law in the New Testament*. New York: Oxford University Press.

Siri, Joseph.

1980   *Gethsemene: Reflections on the Contemporary Theological Movement*. Chicago: Franciscan Herald.

Skarsaune, Oskar.

1991   *Incarnation—Myth or Fact*. Trans. Trygve R. Skarsten. St. Louis: Concordia.

Sobrino, Jon.

1978   *Christology at the Crossroads*. Maryknoll, NY: Orbis.

Spangler, David.

1978   *Reflections on the Christ*. Glasgow: Findhorn.

Stott, John.

1985   *The Authentic Jesus: The Certainty of Christ in a Skeptical World*. Downers Grove, Ill.: InterVarsity.

Stuhlmacher, Peter.

1988   *Jesus von Nazareth—Christus des Glaubens*. Stuttgart: Calver.

Tapia, Ralph J.
1971   *The Theology of Christ: Commentary, Readings in Chris-
        tology.* New York: Bruce.

Tavard, George.
1962   *Paul Tillich and the Christian Message.* New York:
        Scribner's.

Temple, William.
1934   *Nature, Man and God.* Gifford Lectures (1932-34). New
        York: St. Martin's.

Teselle, Eugene.
1975   *Christ in Context.* Philadelphia: Fortress.

Thiemann, Ronald F.
1985   *Revelation and Theology: The Gospel as Narrated Prom-
        ise.* Notre Dame, Ind.: University of Notre Dame Press.

Thorton, Lionel S.
1928   *The Incarnate Lord.* New York: Longmans, Green.

Tillich, Paul.
1951-63 *Systematic Theology.* 3 vols. Chicago: University of Chicago
        Press.

Tupper, E. Frank.
1971   *The Theology of Wolfhart Pannenberg.* Philadelphia:
        Westminster.

Vahanian, Gabriel N.
1961   *The Death of God.* New York: Barziller.

Van Buren, Paul.
1963   *The Secular Meaning of the Gospel.* New York: Macmillan.
1980   *Discerning the Way.* New York: Seabury.

Vermes, Geza.

1987   "Jesus and Christianity" in *Renewing the Judeo-Christian Wellsprings*. Ed. Val Ambrose McInnes. New York: Crossroad.

Wainwright, Geoffrey.

1980   *Doxology: The Praise of God in Worship, Doctrine and Life*. New York: Oxford University Press.

Waldrop, Charles.

1981   "Karl Barth's Concept of the Divinity of Jesus Christ." *Harvard Theological Review* 74:3: 241-53.

Walsh, Michael.

1986   *The Triumph of the Meek: Why Early Christianity Succeeded*. San Francisco: Harper & Row.

Warfield, B. B.

1929   *Christology and Criticism*. New York: Oxford University Press.

Waycock, E. A.

1963   *The Man Who Was Orthodox*. London: Dobson.

Webster, Douglas. A.

1987   *A Passion for Christ: An Evangelical Christology*. Grand Rapids: Zondervan.

Wells, David.

1984   *The Person of Christ*. Westchester, Ill.: Crossway.

Westermann, Claus.

1980   *The Psalms: Structure, Content and Message*. Trans. Ralph D. Gehrke. Minneapolis: Augsburg.

White, John.

1989   "Jesus and the Idea of the New Age." *The Quest*.

Wiles, Maurice.
1967   *The Making of Christian Doctrine*. Cambridge: Cambridge
         University Press.
1976   *Working Papers in Doctrine*. London: SCM.

Williams, Trevor.
1958   *Form and Vitality in God and the World*. Nashville:
         Abingdon.

Willis, Waite W., Jr.
1987   *Theism, Atheism and the Doctrine of the Trinity*. Atlanta:
         Scholars.

Wood, Charles M.
1981   *The Formation of Christian Understanding: An Essay in
         Theological Hermeneutics*. Philadelphia: Westminster.

Woods, G. F.
1965   "The Evidential Value of Biblical Miracles" in *Miracles,
         Cambridge Studies in Their Philosophy and History*. Ed.
         C. F. D. Moule. London: A. R. Mowbray; New York:
         Morehouse-Barlow.

CARL F. H. HENRY was born in New York City in 1913, the decendant of German immigrants. He holds degrees from Wheaton College, Northern Baptist Theological Seminary, and Boston University. He was ordained to the gospel ministry in 1941. In 1947 he helped to found Fuller Theological Seminary in Pasadena, California, and served on its faculty for nine years.

In 1956, Dr. Henry became the founding editor of *Christianity Today.* After twelve years as the magazine's editor, he continued as editor-at-large until 1977. Since then he has had an incredibly productive ministry as author and lecturer. For many years he was a lecturer-at-large for World Vision, and presently he serves in the same capacity for Prison Fellowship.

Since 1941, Dr. Henry has published nearly forty volumes including his magisterial *God, Revelation, and Authority* (1983) which has been called "the most important work of evangelical theology in our times." Samuel Hugh Moffett, Professor Emeritus at Princeton Theological Seminary, has summed up the approach which characterizes Henry's vast literary output: "He is both uncompromising and irenic, socially passionate and evangelistically committed, pastoral and intellectual—and those are rare combinations in today's increasingly polarized societies."